The Visual Artist
and the Law

Associated Councils of the Arts
The Association of the Bar of the
City of New York
Volunteer Lawyers for the Arts

Arts Law Study 1

The Praeger Special Studies program—utilizing the most modern and efficient book production techniques and a selective worldwide distribution network—makes available to the academic, government, and business communities significant, timely research in U.S. and international economic, social, and political development.

The Visual Artist and the Law

Revised Edition

Praeger Publishers   New York   Washington   London

PRAEGER SPECIAL STUDIES IN U.S. ECONOMIC, SOCIAL, AND POLITICAL ISSUES

Library of Congress Cataloging in Publication Data

Main entry under title:

The Visual artist and the law.

(Praeger special studies in U.S. economic, social, and political issues. Arts law study 1)
1. Law and art. I. Associated Councils of the Arts. II. Association of the Bar of the City of New York. III. Volunteer Lawyers for the Arts.
KF390.A7V56   1974   344'.73'097   73-19830

PRAEGER PUBLISHERS
111 Fourth Avenue, New York, N.Y. 10003, U.S.A.

Published in the United States of America in 1974
by Praeger Publishers, Inc.

Second printing, 1976

Printed in the United States of America

Paperback cover design by Frank Mouris

ACKNOWLEDGMENTS
TO THE SECOND EDITION

As with the First Edition, preparation of this revised Second Edition was a collaborative effort, involving the cooperation of knowledgeable and enthusiastic professionals.

All revisions were co-ordinated by Hanno Mott, Chairman of the Art Committee of The Association of the Bar of the City of New York, Howard N. Lefkowitz, a member of that Committee, and William P. Kosmas, Executive Director of Volunteer Lawyers for the Arts. Manufacturing and publication matters were supervised by Anne Wadsworth, Director of Programs at Associated Councils of the Arts. Substantive revisions were made by Haskell Edelstein (Taxes), Carl L. Zanger (Copyright), and Richard S. Scanlon (Miscellaneous Legislation in the Field), all of whom are members of the Art Committee of The Association of the Bar of the City of New York, and by Robert A. Gorman (Copyright), Professor of law, University of Pennsylvania Law School. Charles N. Burger, Eric van Ginkel and Anthony P. Limitone, VLA volunteers, updated and checked the footnotes.

PREFACE
TO THE SECOND EDITION
Paul H. Epstein

This revised edition of *The Visual Artist and the Law* is the first of a number of studies relating to Arts Law which Volunteer Lawyers for the Arts will publish within the Praeger Special Studies series.

The response to the first edition of *The Visual Artist and the Law* was so enthusiastic that it made clear—not only the need for another edition of the book—but the need for many similar books to introduce artists to other problems they face, as well as to assist arts lawyers in meeting the needs of the arts community.

We remain deeply grateful to the Art Committee of the Association of the Bar of the City of New York and to Associated Counsels of the Arts for their efforts in making possible *The Visual Artist and the Law.* We are also grateful to the National Endowment for the Arts, the New York State Council on the Arts, the Rockefeller Family Fund and the J. M. Kaplan Fund for their support during the preparation of this volume.

P.H.E.

ACKNOWLEDGMENTS
TO THE FIRST EDITION

The collaborative effort was facilitated by the assistance given by certain knowledgeable and enthusiastic professionals, some in law, some in the arts. Howard N. Lefkowitz of the Art Committee of The Association of the Bar coordinated the preparation and assisted in the organization and editing of the materials; Stephen E. Weil, administrator of The Whitney Museum of Art, offered various constructive suggestions to the chapters on The Artist and his Gallery and The Artist and the Museum; Miriam G. Cedarbaum of the Museum of Modern Art was helpful with respect to The Artist and the Museum; Clare Romano, president of The American Society of Graphic Artists, and Joseph Rothman, formerly assistant attorney general of the State of New York, both provided useful comments with respect to The Artist and his Galley; Harold S. Klein, on behalf of The Committee of Copyright and Literary Property of The Association of the Bar, was particularly instructive with respect to the Copyright chapter; George Barnett of the Art Committee of The Association of the Bar was generous with his time and prepared the basic material for the chapter on Tax Problems of the Artist; Janet E. Gracey, publication manager of Associated Councils of the Arts, provided superb assistance with the editing and preparation of the manuscript for publication; and Joseph Farrell, former vice president of Associated Councils of the Arts, Jan Ellen Rein, former executive director of Volunteer Lawyers for the Arts and Paul B. DeWitt, executive secretary of The Association of the Bar, furnished advice and encouragement. The officers and directors of Volunteer Lawyers for the Arts provided assistance with the editing.

A substantial part of the essential labor was performed by five lawyers of the Volunteer Lawyers for the Arts: Thomas L. Creel (Copyright); Barry D. Rein (The Artist and his Gallery); Burton D. Hunter (The Artist and the Museum); Michael A. Nayor (The Artist and the Publisher; Studio Sales and Commissioned Works); and Wade S. Hooker, Jr. (Content and Structure of Art Works).

The need for this monograph was first suggested in May 1969 at a conference sponsored by Associated Councils of the Arts in Quebec, Canada. It was felt that artists sorely needed a publication that would treat some of the various legal problems they encountered. It took, however, a happy alliance among the Art Committee of The Association of the Bar of the City of New York, Volunteer Lawyers for the Arts, and Associated Councils of the Arts to carry the project to fruition. As the oldest (and probably to this day the only) Art Committee of a bar association, this Committee assumed the responsibility, partly out of interest, partly out of devotion, to see that this badly needed project was produced in a manner useful not only to the working artist but also to the lawyer called upon to represent the visual artist in his myriad legal relationships. Volunteer Lawyers for the Arts, reacting with refreshing enthusiasm, supplied the lawyers who produced a substantial part of the manuscript. Associated Councils of the Arts furnished the counsel and publication wherewithal to insure that the project would become a reality. Without the cooperation of the three organizations, this project would not have been completed.

We have tried to make the monograph useful to both the artist and the lawyer. Often this has meant a sacrifice of simplicity for precision. The various problems that are treated do not, unfortunately, always have clear-cut answers. It is hoped, however, that this publication will inform the artist of significant legal problems he may encounter and increase his sensitivity to the issues and possible solutions, and that it will apprise the lawyer of the fascinating issues that have existed and continue to persist in the creative life of the visual artist.

Franklin Feldman
Chairman, Art Committee
The Association of the Bar
of the City of New York

CONTENTS

INTRODUCTION

This work deals with the legal problems of the visual artist. The term visual artist is intended to cover any creator of a work of painting, drawing, graphic art, and sculpture. The focus is on the working artist: the person attempting to support himself exclusively through the creation of his personal product. The monograph also deals with certain laws, which only incidentally affect the artist, that are of principal concern to others in the art field: the art collector, art dealer, and authenticator of fine art. While the material is directed to the creation of a work of fine art, many of the laws and principles discussed apply equally to the work product of the commercial artist.

The monograph is not intended to cover other "artists," particularly those in the performing arts, such as singers, dancers, musicians and the like, although some of the principles discussed would apply to other art forms. For example, the sections dealing with copyright and right of reproduction would apply to the photographer. Similarly, the subject matter is not immediately concerned with other forms of the visual arts that have problems peculiar to themselves, such as motion pictures, video cassettes, tapes, and cartridges.

No attempt has been made to provide standard or recommended forms. Indeed, no single type of form exists to cover all situations, and the precise agreement used in a particular case must depend on the particular facts (and undoubtedly bargaining power) that exist. Rather, the emphasis has been to isolate problems frequently encountered by visual artists in their varied commercial relationships and to suggest solutions that should be given consideration. Needless to say, the artist's own lawyer should be consulted if any serious negotiation is contemplated.

One further caveat: this monograph does not purport to be a definitive work on the problems it treats; it does, however, attempt to deal with most of the problems likely to confront the visual artist in his commercial and other legal relationships.

The Visual Artist
and the Law

Despite artists' claims to uniqueness and individualistic reaction to stimuli, it is paradoxical that they approach one important matter with indiscriminate uniformity and, from a legal point of view, outright foolishness. With the rarest of exceptions,* famous as well as struggling artists do not take the minimal formal step that would protect their work from copying or reproduction by others—that is, they do not "copyright."

Whether the failure to secure protection under the Federal Copyright Law is based on the belief that to do so would be unduly "commerical," or that placing the copyright notice on the work might detract from its beauty, or because of lack of knowledge on the part of artists, the result is the same in every case—unless copyright protection is secured when the work is "published," all rights in the work are lost forever.

The failure to take the few simple steps needed to secure statutory copyright of the monumental *Chicago Picasso* sculpture resulted recently in the loss of all protection for the work.[1] Anyone is free to exploit the work commercially for his own private benefit (for example, by making copies of the work or sale of picture postcards of it) without paying anything to the artist or to the Art Institute of Chicago which owns the work.

In general, copyright laws protect against any unauthorized use or copying of all or a substantial portion of a work.[2] Prior to publication a work is protected automatically under the 'common law' (i.e. case law) of the several states. Once publication occurs, however, unless the minimal steps are taken which are required to secure protection under the Federal Copyright Laws

---

*One noteworthy exception is the leading graphic artist, Robert Indiana, creator of the serigraph "LOVE" that undoubtedly has inspired many commercial by-products, who recently has added the requisite copyright notice to his work in a departure from his prior practice.

1

(and, where appropriate, under copyright treaties or 'Conventions' with foreign nations) all rights in the work are lost.

"Publication" in the technical copyright sense means making the work available to the general public without any restrictions or limitations as to the use which the public can make of the work.[3] Prior to publication there is no limit to the duration of common law copyright protection. However, under the Federal Copyright Statute, a work is protected for an original term of 28 years from publication and may be protected for one renewal term of 28 years by applying for renewal during the last year of the initial copyright term.[4]

Many textbooks discussing copyright are available,[5] so it is intended here briefly to acquaint the artist with the means of protecting his work through the copyright laws and the rights he acquires under copyright in as simplified a form as possible.

COPYRIGHT COVERAGE

Almost any work coming within the scope of this monograph is eligible for copyright protection.[6] For example, drawings, photographs, paintings, etchings, sculpture, and artistic jewelry are covered.

Illustrations in books, cuts, pictures, books of pictures, illustrations, cartoons, etcetera, are also eligible.

There are special statutory provisions which relate principally to books written in the English language which have only a limited bearing on copyright protection for works of art. These relate to the content of the copyright notice (a special abbreviated form of copyright notice is provided for works of art[7]) where the notice must appear (in the case of a printed work, on the title page or the page immediately following[8]) and where the printing process must take place (generally within the limits of the United States, with certain exceptions[9]).

Since these details are complex, attorneys familiar with such requirements should be consulted if a book or other printed publication is contemplated.

Special rules limit the availability and extent of copyright protection of works of art in the following situations:

a) An independent work of an identical or similar nature that is not copied from a pre-existing copyrighted work does not infringe that work and may itself be independently copyrighted. Two photographers or painters, for example, might use the same source material and produce remarkably similar end products, but only the *artistic* content of the copyrighted work is protected, as anyone is free to use the same source material and render his own artistic impression of it.[10]

b) Similarly, one who bases his work on an underlying theme embodied in an already copyrighted work does not infringe that work.[11] For example, if there were a series of panels depicting Russian peasant life in the early 1900's, another could do his own impression in panels of this same period and there would not be protection available for the first artist against the second.

c) Titles of works are normally not protected by copyright.[12] However, under the unfair competition or trademark laws (and not the patent or copyright laws) certain titles that have come to be identified with a particular source—such as the title "L'l Abner" for the comic strip by Al Capp—may be protected, and Mr. Capp could probably prevent another from using that title.

d) Strictly functional items such as tools that have no artistic value are not subject to copyright.[13] Copyright covers only an artist's artistic expression as embodied in a work of art.

e) Works of art *other than* by United States citizens or foreign nationals who live permanently in the United States.[14] Foreign artists who initially obtained copyright protection in their own countries are protected in the United States, either under international conventions, if their country and the United States are both party to the same convention, or under Presidential proclamations which extend the benefit of United States copyright protection to nationals of specific countries on a reciprocal basis. Published works of foreign origin must have a complete international form of copyright notice, including the symbol © and the name of the copyright proprietor and the year of first publication, in order to be protected in the United States.

f) Lithographs or photoengravings. Lithographs or photoengravings by American artists *must* be printed in the United States in order to be protected under the U.S. Copyright Law. The only exception is if the subjects represented are located in a foreign country and illustrate a scientific work or reproduce a work of art. This requirement applies both to illustrations included in a book in the English language or written by an American national, as well as to separate lithographs and photoengravings.[15]

g) "Fair Use" of copyrighted works.[16] In certain instances, even actual copying of a work may be permitted as a "fair use." For example, where a book reviewer quotes (copies) a few sentences from a book being reviewed, the courts have ruled that such limited copying is allowed, even though no permission was sought or received from the author: (i) since it is usual, reasonable and customary to do so; (ii) because usually only a small portion is reproduced; (iii) such use by the critic is not likely to be used to compete with the copyright proprietor's own work; and (iv) the use by the critic is ancillary to a scholarly or critical analysis. The doctrine is limited principally to written works, but may also apply to works of art. For example, a copy of copyrighted painting included in the background in a published news photo of a public personality might very well be permitted as a "fair use" of the painting. Similarly, the reproduction of a painting in a review of an artist's work may be permissible. Whether or not a limited use is a "fair use" depends upon the particular facts of each case.[17]

WHAT PROTECTION IS AVAILABLE

Copyright, as defined earlier, provides protection against any unauthorized use of copying of all or a substantial portion of the copyrighted work.

Thus, the taking of photographs of a work is prohibited, as is using the work to make an identical copy or a substantially identical work in a different medium. Consequently, copying an oil painting in water color would be a violation of a copyright.

In addition to copyright protection available, in many cases three-dimensional art work can also be protected by design patent. Patent coverage is, however, normally not considered appropriate for fine arts since obtaining a patent is expensive, it entails a protracted period of correspondence with the Patent Office, and because design patents are primarily directed to industrial designs as distinguished from fine art. There is also a difference in the scope and length of coverage. For the purpose of this monograph, only copyright protection will be considered.[18]

Copyrighted works of American origin may be protected abroad under one of several different international arrangements. These differ both as to the countries that are party to them and as to the extent of protection granted under them. The United States and approximately 60 other countries are parties to the Universal Copyright Convention.[19] Under this convention, copyrighted works of nationals of each country are protected in all of the other countries provided the works bear the specified form of international copyright notice consisting of the symbol © plus the name of the copyright proprietor and year of first publication. Although the United States is not a party of the Berne Convention, a work first published in the United States may be protected in the approximately 62 countries that are parties to that treaty if the work is published simultaneously (within 14 to 30 days of first publication) in one of the countries which is a member of the Berne Convention.[20] The United States is also a party to the Buenos Aires Convention,[21] along with 17 Latin American nations, some of which are not parties to any other international copyright treaty. An American work of art will be protected in all of the countries adhering to this convention if it contains a statement indicating that property rights in the work are reserved.

In addition to the multinational conventions, the United States is party to numerous treaties with individual countries granting copyright protection to American artists in those countries and to nationals of those countries in the United States on a reciprocal basis.

A New York State statute provides that whenever a work of fine art—a painting, sculpture, drawing, or work of graphic art—is sold or transferred by the artist who created it or his heirs or personal representatives, the right of reproduction remains with the artist unless such right is specifically transferred by a written instrument, sale contract, or memorandum.[22] "Fair use" of the work, however, is permitted. The right of reproduction is exemplified by reproductions used for greeting cards, on television, in advertising, etcetera, i.e., reproductions that are used for purposes for which publishers customarily pay. However, according to the legislative history of the statute, such "reproduction" by a museum in its exhibition catalogs, slides, post cards, etcetera, is not intended to be covered by the statute. Questions as to the scope of the statute and possible conflict with the federal copyright laws have, however, been raised.*

This statute was intended to regulate only those works not yet published, i.e., those under which a "common law copyright" is claimed. Without such a statute, a single unrestricted sale might also pass the right to reproduce the work to the purchaser, as a New York Court had previously held.[23] Under the United States copyright law, an unrestricted and absolute sale of a work bearing the proper copyright notice does not by itself transfer the copyright and hence the artist still has the right of reproduction after he makes such an unqualified sale;[24] a separate assignment of the copyright would be necessary to transfer this right to the buyer. If the work is published, the federal statute would apply rather than the New York statute.

WHAT CONSTITUTES PUBLICATION

Since the common law copyright ceases and statutory copyright commences at the instant of publication, the definition of "publication" is critical. As defined earlier, publication in the copyright sense means making one or more copies of the work available to the general public without any express or implied restriction or limitation as to the use which the public can make of the work. For instance, unrestricted sale of the original or even one copy may be by itself enough to amount to a publication.[25] Also, exhibition in a gallery or museum where there is no restriction on taking photographs or copying would probably amount to publication.[26] In contrast, limited distribution with restrictions as to use would not waive the common law rights of the artist.[27] For example, sending the work to a museum, gallery, or publisher for approval with instructions that the work is not to be displayed would probably not be publication. There are, however, innumerable situations similar to those just set forth where reasonable men (and hence courts) could differ as to whether or not there was a publication.[28] For that reason it is always preferable to attach a copyright notice immediately when the work is completed to insure that no inadvertent publication destroys all rights.

PRIOR TO PUBLICATION

Common law copyright comes into existence automatically when the work is created, and continues indefinitely without the need for registration or any other formality so long as the work (i) remains unpublished, and (ii) no

---

*See Chapter 8, p. 62 for a discussion of this problem and a more detailed discussion of the statute itself.

statutory copyright protection has been secured for it as an unpublished work. Under this right, the artist may withhold his work or make the first publication of it. He may restrain any unauthorized publication or use of his work, and recover any damages he may have sustained.

The principal weakness of this common law right is that the artist cannot reap any financial rewards from the copying of his work without publication, and at this point the common law right ends.

AT PUBLICATION

Statutory copyright is obtained by publishing the work and giving the public notice of the claim of copyright by placing a notice physically on the work to be protected (not on tags, labels, etcetera, which are removable). If there is no copyright notice on the work at the time it is published, the work enters the public domain and any right covered by the copyright law that the artist may have is forever lost.

Copyright Notice

The form of this notice is mandated by statute[29] and should include three elements:
1) the word "Copyright" or its abbreviation "Copr." or its symbol ©"
2) the name of the copyright proprietor*
3) the year of first publication.[30]

The following form is appropriate: "© John Artist 1971." *This notice must be placed on each original art work and authorized copy at the time of publication or any rights the artist has will be lost.*[31]

The word "copyright" is not specifically required by statute when "©" is used. It is recommended, however, that both be used when the work is to appear in any printed form to avoid problems that frequently occur if they are not. The reason is strictly practical: type-setters sometimes make errors in the setting of the "©" or they do not have the symbol available, and if the symbol is used alone and improperly, all protection is lost.

---

*In works created for hire, i.e., where the artist is on a salary and completion of the work is part of his normal duties, the employer rather than the artist should be named as proprietor in the notice. Also in a commissioned work where the customer initiates the work and pays for it, the customer is normally entitled to be listed as the proprietor in the copyright notice. These details may be covered in the contract with the artist's employer or the person commissioning the work, as discussed in later chapters. If the contract is silent, the artist should be named as the proprietor on the notice. In this case, any errors in naming the proprietor can be corrected later. If two or more persons contributed to the artistic expression of the work, both should be listed as proprietors.

There is a "short form" notice that can be used in the United States on works of art or authorized reproductions—drawings, photographs, and prints and pictorial illustrations, among others.[32] The short form consists of "©JBA", where JBA are the initials, monogram, mark, or symbol of the copyright proprietor. If this form is used, the proprietor's full name must appear in addition on some accessible and visible portion of the work, or on the margin, back, permanent base, pedestal, or substance on which the work is mounted.[33] If there is any possibility that the base could be separated from the work, the notice should always be on the work itself.

Many artists use the short form in order not to detract from the artistic value of their work. The use of this notice, however, is only effective in the United States and the work could be copied freely in other countries, including industrialized countries where an artist would be more likely to profit from granting permission to make copies.* The year may also be omitted so far as domestic protection is concerned, but it is required for foreign coverage.[34] *It is therefore recommended that the longer form notice always be used.* If the artist believes copies of his work may have value in Latin America, the phrase "All Rights Reserved" should be added to the long form notice.[35] This will insure protection there, whereas the long form alone may not.

When a copyright is renewed it must bear the original date, and it would be advisable to include the renewal date; for example: "© John Artist 1930; © renewed John Artist 1958."

Placement on Works

There is no statutory requirement as to placement of the notice on work such as drawings, paintings, graphics, or sculpture. In general, any notice which is on an accessible portion of the work (either the front or back, or visible notice on the margin, permanent mounting—the base, pedestal, selvage or frame) is acceptable.[36] It should, however, be placed in the most conspicuous place possible to give the public adequate notice that a copyright is claimed.[37] For drawings, paintings, and other two-dimensional works, it is suggested that a small notation in the lower-righthand corner would be appropriate.[38] On an oil painting, for example, the notice could be painted in and combined with the artist's signature (provided it is legible). On three-dimensional works that are portable and easily handled, the notice could be on the base, providing the base is permanently attached to the work. For larger works, the notice should not be on the base but should be within sight of the ordinary viewer.[39]

---

*The short form notice is not effective under the Universal Copyright Convention since Art. III (1) requires that "from the time of the first publication all the copies of the work published with the authority of the author or other copyright proprietor bear the symbol © accompanied by the name of the copyright proprietor and the year of first publication placed in such manner and location as to give reasonable notice of claim of copyright."

On printed publications or books, the copyright notice *must* be placed on the title page or the page immediately following the title page. In a publication containing the artist's illustrations, cuts, or pictures and additional materials by others, a copyright notice should be attached to each separate item of the artist's work. If such works appear in the book without any notice at all on them, the law is unclear whether the publisher's notice in the front of the book is sufficient to protect each such work therein, and if it is, whether the copyright belongs to the publisher or the artist himself.[40] The problem is that the copyright law requires the notice to be in the name of the "proprietor."

Registration of Copyright

No rights will be lost by not registering the artist's claim to copyright.[41] The rights arise fullblown out of the proper notice. Whether or not the artist decides to register the copyright is a question he must decide himself. Registering the copyright is necessary to enforce the rights obtained by copyrighting, or in renewing the copyright. At either of these times, however, a lawyer should be consulted to retain registration if it has not been done.

The copyright law provides for filing certain documents with the Copyright Office and for payment of minimal fees to secure registration of the claim to copyright.[42] These documents, which can be obtained by writing to the Copyright Office, are quite simple and can be completed by the artist himself. (A sample form appears on pages 10-13.)

For types of work covered by this monograph, the appropriate forms would be: Form G—work of art, model or design; Form H—reproduction of a work of art; Form I—drawing or plastic work of a scientific or technical character; Form J—photographs; Form K—print or pictorial illustration; and Form R—renewal of copyright.

The law provides that two copies of the work must be included with the application,[43] but in cases where the work is expensive, large, extremely heavy, or fragile—as in the case of a painting or sculpture—photographs may be sent instead of actual copies.[44] The copies may be mailed free by taking them to the Post Office where the sender will receive a receipt.[45]

Transfer of Rights

The right to reproduce either a copyrighted or uncopyrighted work can be passed by contract at the time of sale or at any time. Whether or not the reproduction rights are transferred depends solely upon the language in the contract. The artist should, therefore, be particularly careful of the language used in transferring his work.

An assignment of a statutory copyright must be in writing and signed by the proprietor,[46] but a common law copyright can be orally assigned.[47] Written documents evidencing such assignments must be filed with the Copyright Office to enable the first purchaser to have superior rights over a second purchaser from the same seller who did not have actual notice of the first sale.[48] The recordation of the assignment must be accomplished within three months after the assignment's execution, if executed within the United States, or within six months if executed outside the United States.[49] A statutory copyright may also be bequeathed by a Will.[50]

PROPOSED REVISION OF COPYRIGHT LAW

Copyright revision bills have been before Congress for almost a decade. Chances of passage of the general copyright revision bill now pending in Congress are slim, but most persons experienced in the field recognize that there is a need for revision of the provisions and some bill will no doubt be passed in the future. This section is intended to alert the artist to the fact that the advice given above is not immutable and that changes can, and probably will, occur. Selected features of the pending bill are summarized below, with particular emphasis on those provisions affecting works of art.

The bill (S. 1361 introduced by Senator McClellan, chairman of the Patents, Trademarks and Copyrights Subcommittee, on March 26, 1973) generally has three major subdivisions (titles): the first title is a general revision of the copyright statutes and procedures; Title II provides for establishment in the Library of Congress of a national commission on new technological uses of copyrighted works; and Title III provides for the protection of ornamental designs of useful articles.

One of the major proposals is the abolition of the dual system of copyright: statutory copyright after publication and common law copyright before publication. Also, the term of copyright would be changed from 28 years plus a renewal term of 28 years to the life of the author plus 50 years after his death; the areas in which the short form notice may be used are narrowed; and, under certain circumstances, the bill would prevent an omission of or defect in a copyright notice from thrusting the work into the public domain.

The bill provides for the first statutory recognition of the "fair use" doctrine, and specifies that the "fair use" of a copyrighted work, including reproduction for purposes of teaching or research, does not amount to copyright infringement. The bill also provides that under certain conditions reproduction by libraries and archives does not amount to infringement. With copyrighted pictorial, graphic, or sculptured work that has been reproduced in useful articles and distributed to the public, there is no infringement by the use of photographs in connection with advertisements or commentaries relating to the articles or in news reports.

Page 1

FORM G

CLASS	REGISTRATION NO.
G	DO NOT WRITE HERE
	GF GU
	GFO GP

Application for Registration of a Claim to Copyright
in a work of art or a model or design for a work of art

Instructions: Make sure that all applicable spaces have been completed before you submit the form. The application must be **SIGNED** at line 11. For published works the application should not be submitted until after the date of publication given in line 6(a), and should state the facts which existed on that date. For further information, see page 4.

Pages 1 and 2 should be typewritten or printed with pen and ink. Pages 3 and 4 should contain exactly the same information as pages 1 and 2, but may be carbon copies.

Mail all pages of the application to the **Register of Copyrights**, Library of Congress, Washington, D.C. 20540, together with:

(a) If unpublished, a photograph or other identifying reproduction of the work and the registration fee of **$6.**

(b) If published, two copies of the best edition of the work (or if appropriate, photographs—see line 4) and the registration fee of **$6.**

Make your remittance payable to the **Register of Copyrights.**

1. Copyright Claimant(s) and Address(es): Give the name(s) and address(es) of the copyright owner(s). For published works the name(s) should ordinarily be the same as in the notice of copyright on the copies deposited. If initials are used in the notice, the name should be the same as appears elsewhere on the copies.

Name .... John Artist ....

Address .... 1111 E. 4th Street, New York, New York 10038 ....

Name ....

Address ....

2. Title: .... Man Sitting On Pedestal ....
(Give the title of the work as it appears on the copies; a descriptive title may be used where the work is entirely pictorial or sculptural)

3. Nature of Work: .... Sculpture ....
(Characterize the general type of artistic work involved, as, for example, painting, drawing, sculpture, design, model, etc.)

➤➤ **NOTE:** Leave line 4 blank unless the work has been **PUBLISHED and photographs deposited in lieu of copies.** ◄

4. Optional Deposit: (See information on page 4.)

Basis for claiming option (Check and fill in **ONE** of the following):

☐ Monetary value (retail value per copy) ....

☐ Size (give dimensions) ....

☐ Fragility (give details) ....

☐ Weight (in pounds) ....

5. Author (i.e., Artist): Citizenship and domicile information must be given. Where a work is made for hire, the employer is the author. The citizenship of organizations formed under U.S. Federal or State law should be stated as U.S.A. If the copyright claim is based on new matter (see line 7) **give** information about the author of new matter.

Name ...... John Artist .... Citizenship ...... U.S.A. ......

(Give legal name followed by pseudonym if latter appears on the copies)   (Name of country)

Domiciled in U.S.A. Yes .. X .. No ...... Address .. 1111 E. 4th Street, New York, N.Y. 10033

➤ NOTE: **Leave all spaces of line 6 blank unless your work has been PUBLISHED.** ◄━

6. (a) Date of Publication: Give the complete date when copies of this particular work were first placed on sale, sold, or publicly distributed. The date when copies were made or printed should not be confused with the date of publication. NOTE: The full date (month, day, and year) must be given.

June 21 1971

(Month)   (Day)   (Year)

(b) Place of Publication: Give the name of the country in which this particular work was first published.

United States

(c) Manufacture Outside United States by Lithographic or Photoengraving Process: If the copies of this work were manufactured outside the United States by lithographic or photoengraving process, give the name of the country of manufacture.

➤ NOTE: **Leave all spaces of line 7 blank unless the instructions below apply to your work.** ◄━

7. Previous Registration or Publication: If a claim to copyright in any substantial part of this work was previously registered in the U.S. Copyright Office in unpublished form, or if a substantial part of the work was previously published anywhere, give requested information.

Was work previously registered? Yes ...... No .X. Date of registration .... Registration number ....

Was work previously published? Yes ...... No .X. Date of publication .... Registration number ....

Is there any substantial **NEW MATTER** in this version? Yes ...... No ...... If your answer is "Yes," give a brief general statement of the nature of the **NEW MATTER** in this version. (New matter may consist of compilation, abridgment, editorial revision, and the like, as well as additional artistic or graphic material.)

EXAMINER

Complete all applicable spaces on next page

8. If registration fee is to be charged to a deposit account established in the Copyright Office, give name of account:

9. Name and address of person or organization to whom correspondence or refund, if any, should be sent:

Name .... John Artist .... Address .... 1111 E. 4th Street, New York, N.Y. ....

10. Send certificate to:

(Type or print name and address)

Name John Artist

Address 1111 E. 4th Street
    (Number and street)

New York New York 10038
(City)   (State)   (ZIP code)

11. Certification:

(Application not acceptable unless signed)

I CERTIFY that the statements made by me in this application are correct to the best of my knowledge.

☞ *John Artist*
    (Signature of copyright claimant or duly authorized agent)

Application Forms

Copies of the following forms will be supplied by the Copyright Office without charge upon request.

Class A Form A—Published book manufactured in the United States of America.

Class A or B Form A–B Foreign—Book or periodical manufactured outside the United States of America (except works subject to the ad interim provisions of the copyright law).

Form A–B Ad Interim—Book or periodical in the English language manufactured and first published outside the United States of America.

Class B { Form B—Periodical manufactured in the United States of America.
Form BB—Contribution to a periodical manufactured in the United States of America.

Class C   Form C—Lecture or similar production prepared for oral delivery.

Class D   Form D—Dramatic or dramatico-musical composition.

Form E—Musical composition the author of which is a citizen or domiciliary of the United States of America or which was first published in the United States of America.

Class E { Form E Foreign—Musical composition the author of which is not a citizen or domiciliary of the United States of America and which was not first published in the United States of America.

Class F   Form F—Map.

Class G   Form G—Work of art or a model or design for a work of art.

Class H   Form H—Reproduction of a work of art.

Class I   Form I—Drawing or plastic work of a scientific or technical character.

Class J   Form J—Photograph.

Class K { Form K—Print or pictorial illustration.
Form KK—Print or label used for an article of merchandise.

Class L
or M { Form L–M—Motion picture.

Form R—Renewal copyright.

Form U—Notice of use of copyrighted music on mechanical instruments.

FOR COPYRIGHT OFFICE USE ONLY		
Application received	Two copies received	Photographs or reproductions received
One copy or reproduction received		
Fee received		
Renewal		

U S GOVERNMENT PRINTING OFFICE 1970 O—369–590

Page 2

Title II of the bill, the establishment of the national commission, provides that the commission is to study and compile data on the reproduction and use of copyrighted work in automatic systems capable of storing, processing, retrieving, and transferring information (computer programs) and in various forms of machine reproduction.

Title III would offer creators of ornamental designs of useful objects a new form of protection intended to avoid the defects of existing copyright and design patent statutes by providing simple, easily-secured and effective protection for such designs for a period of either 5 or 10 years.

2

THE ARTIST AND
HIS GALLERY

The gallery is the artist's window to the buying public. Ideally, the gallery takes on the tasks of creating a market for the artist's works by showing and publicizing them, and selling them. The artist is left free for creative effort, unburdened by problems of marketing his works, and undisturbed by a procession of prospective purchasers tramping through his studio.

In practice, the gallery cannot completely divorce itself from artistic problems, and the artist must be aware of the gallery's commercial milieu in order both to negotiate a satisfactory agreement and to facilitate a productive working relationship. This chapter attempts to promote such an awareness, rather than give the reader an in-depth knowledge of all potential legal problems inherent in the relationship.[1]

TYPES OF GALLERIES

Galleries most commonly combine two distinct operations under a single roof. In one, works belonging not to the gallery, but to individual artists under contract with the gallery, are exhibited for sale. The gallery is acting as the artist's agent, or representative. In the other, the gallery acts as a dealer—buying and selling for its own account. The former case usually involves works of living artists; the latter may customarily include works of artists living or long dead. While usually less profitable to the gallery, its sales in an agency capacity lend a sense of currency that attracts business. New York has recently enacted a statute which provides that "any custom, practice or usage of the trade to the contrary notwithstanding . . . whenever an artist delivers . . . a work of fine art of his own creation to an art dealer for the purpose of exhibition and/or sale on a commission, fee or other basis of compensation, the delivery to and acceptance thereof by the art dealer is deemed to be 'on consignment.' "[2] That is to say, absent an express agreement providing for immediate sale of the artist's work to the gallery, the statute treats the gallery as the agent of the artist.

As the artist's agent, the gallery is charged with selling works consigned to it, i.e., works in which the artist retains title, or ownership; the gallery has the right to possession, the right to pass title to purchasers, and related rights and duties mutually agreed upon as necessary or valuable to its task. The purpose of the agreement between artist and gallery is to define their respective rights and obligations regarding consigned works and related matters. The areas of potential conflict arising out of this relationship that should be covered in an agreement are covered separately in the following paragraphs. The content of specific provisions will be determined by bargaining between the parties in each actual case.

THE AGREEMENT

An agreement often will not contain provisions for all of the potential conflict areas described below; and additional areas not discussed here may be covered. In each case, the agreement should respond to the parties' peculiar needs and situations. If an agreement is silent on a particular question, that silence often has legal effect as to what the parties may have intended. There are no hard and fast rules governing how an artist and gallery get together for the first time. The script is written anew each time. Contact may be initiated either by the artist or the gallery.

Sometimes a gallery will offer an annual stipend, so that the artist has the burden of everyday subsistence lifted from him, to be repaid in the artist's works. While superficially attractive, this kind of advance arrangement should be carefully considered, for reasons explained later.

Ordinarily, a written contract, especially one negotiated or reviewed by lawyers for both sides, is preferred to an oral understanding sealed by a handshake. An oral agreement can be enforced if for a term less than one year and if the works to be shown or sold, price, and other essential terms are agreed upon. But more often than not, the terms of an oral agreement cannot accurately be recalled, let alone proven, so that a written agreement is greatly preferred. The problem areas most often encountered—and which should be covered in an agreement—are treated below.

Identity of the Parties

One naturally tends at the outset to make certain assumptions about the gallery, for example that it will not move from its chic, Madison Avenue location to Elmhurst during the contract term, or that the luminary whose reputation sustains the gallery will not leave and enter into competition with it. While usually sound, assumptions of this kind should be backed up by express undertakings. While the artist cannot (and should not) ordinarily dictate the conduct of the gallery's business, he can at least contract to terminate his own obligations to the gallery upon the occurrence of unwanted events of sufficient magnitude.

If participation by certain individuals in the gallery's management are important to the artist, they should be named in the agreement. Especially if the gallery is a corporation, an important individual may be asked to personally sign the agreement, containing appropriate representations assuring his continued personal participation. The nature of the gallery, whether a corporation, partnership, voluntary association, or other business entity, should be specified. Whether or not corporate in form, the gallery might be sold or merged and thereby lose its character and identity during the contract term. The artist may wish to have the option to terminate in such event.

From the gallery's point of view, the location of the artist's studio may be important. If the gallery desires to review the artist's output periodically, to choose work for exhibition or sale, it may well want to limit location of the studio (and thus its own travel) to a reasonable radius.

Scope of the Agreement

The scope of the agreement, in geography, time, kinds of works, proportion of the artist's output, and other important dimensions, must be clearly specified.

The gallery's authority may extend geographically to the entire world, or may be limited to a single city. A New York gallery may have branches in Paris and London but not in Boston or on the West Coast, permitting representation by a different gallery in the latter locations. Thus to an extent, the geographic scope of the agreement will follow that of the gallery. However, the gallery may have an established clientele in a city where it has no branch, but sells by distribution of photographs of its artists' works. The gallery would generally want exclusive rights in such a city.

Further questions may arise as to operation of the geographic limitation. For example, an artist may have a New York gallery with a Paris branch, and a separate and independent San Francisco gallery. For a sale to a San Francisco resident on holiday in Paris, by the Paris gallery, is the San Francisco gallery entitled to a commission? Probably not, but the possibility should be borne in mind in drafting the agreemen .

Any agreement has numerous dimensions, the scope of which may require definition. The kinds of work covered by the agreement should be defined. If a painter takes up needlepoint several months after signing a contract covering "all artistic works," the gallery may well be entitled to his first set of chair cushions. Whether limited to representational paintings or comprehending all works, the type of works intended to be covered should be specified.

Commissioned works may be excluded from the scope of the agreement, reflecting the fact that they are based more directly on the artist's reputation, and not so much on any display seen in the gallery. To the extent that an artist's reputation is enhanced through the efforts of his gallery, the gallery can logically expect to share payment for commissioned works. Nevertheless, a line can rationally be drawn, and such works excluded from the agreement.

The agreement should be limited in time. It may be for one year, or several years, or a shorter period. The term should not be too long, simply because most factors important to both parties become less predictable the longer the period. Provision for a term greater than three years should be scrutinized carefully to see if it is really advantageous. Usually an option to renew granted to one party is a more flexible arrangement than one for an unduly long term. To whom the option is granted depends on the desires and bargaining power of the parties. A gallery may extend an unknown artist a one-year contract, reserving the right to renew on the same terms for two successive one-year periods. An artist of greater repute may himself be given an option to renew after an initial period. Naturally, the parties can terminate by mutual consent at any time.

In view of the close cooperation between artist and gallery necessary for a successful relationship, it may be desirable in some cases to permit either party to terminate on 30 or 60 days notice. If the artist terminates in this manner, he may be required to reimburse the gallery for any recent large expenditures, such as the cost of an exhibit. Contract terms longer than five years are unusual.

As a practical matter a gallery can almost always terminate the relationship by simply not promoting the artist's work as originally contemplated. Hence, precise contractual provisions for termination of the agreement are essential for the artist's benefit.

A question closely related to the type of works to be covered is the portion of the artist's output to be included. The gallery may be entitled to the artist's entire output, or it may only be entitled to one work. The gallery may be granted the right to select a given number of works annually, or selection of the works may be left to the artist. Or the gallery may select the first twenty and the artist the next twenty, for example. Since the gallery can be expected to know its clients' tastes better than the artist, it ordinarily reserves the right to make the selection if less than the entire output is covered.

Whatever proportion of the artist's output is covered, if less than all, there remains the question whether and to what extent he can dispose of his own works through other channels, sometimes felt to be natural exceptions to gallery sales. Studio sales are the principal exception, and provision should be made for some mutually acceptable number of them. Gifts are another exception and should be expressly provided for if the artist desires to make them, even though no money is involved. A third such exception is the use of the artist's works for barter. The artist's right to retain works for himself or to bequeath works to others (if the contract binds his estate) may also be subject to limitation. All such methods may be lumped together, for example, in a provision for excepting up to an agreed number per year of works from those due the gallery.

Artistic Control

Serious disputes may arise over how and where the artist's works are shown and distributed by the gallery, unless some agreement is made at the outset.

It might be upsetting to see one's latest canvas adorning a soap powder advertisement, or hung with works of (in the artist's view) a less talented artist. An artist of a particular political persuasion may not want to be exhibited for the benefit of an opposing political party. He may not wish the gallery to supply photographs of his works to illustrate a magazine article damning him.

The gallery, on the other hand, may not share the artist's artistic or other sensibilities, and may simply want to maximize profits. To reconcile the two sometimes conflicting views, the artist should at least have the right to be consulted with respect to all gallery and museum exhibitions, publicity, and other distribution and exhibition of his works. Under circumstances deemed most important to him, he may request and obtain a veto power over any action proposed by the gallery. With respect to decisions considered less important, the mere requirement for consultation will usually prevent sharp disagreements.

A related question of artistic control arises with respect to works in the hands of a purchaser from the gallery. If the artist for some reason refuses to sell a work to a purchaser residing in the Midwest, it must be spelled out in the contract. More reasonably, he may desire the right to regain temporary possession of certain works every five years for exhibition, or to control the manner of exhibition whenever the work is exhibited by the purchaser. Reservation by the artist of limited artistic control after sale has been suggested with increasing frequency in recent years, and artists should not hesitate to request it. Such control must be expressed both in the agreement between artist and gallery, and in each bill of sale from gallery to purchaser.

Exhibitions

An artist needs exposure to the public in order to sell, and part of the gallery's undertaking is ordinarily to provide such exposure by way of exhibits and efforts to arrange museum shows, with appropriate publicity. However, there are no specific requirements for exhibits, openings, or any other form of publicity implicit in the mere signing of an agreement; the expected arrangements must be spelled out.

If one or more exhibit is to be provided, the location, date, duration and amount of space should be agreed upon. The artist will probably want to have some say in arranging, hanging, and lighting his works; the gallery is probably paying the bills so it will want enough control to limit costs. If the exhibit includes several artists, questions of artistic control become more complex, e.g., the relative placement of the various artists' works. Presumably, the artist will at least wish to be consulted about other artists in the same show, and perhaps reserve the right to approve them.

Elementary questions, such as who pays the champagne bill and for how much, should be generally agreed upon beforehand. Some control over the format and content of advertising and catalogs may be retained by the artist, while the gallery will probably want to control the budget (unless the artist is paying for them) and certain stylistic factors. Other questions to be considered include whether or not the show may be a benefit, the minimum amount to be spent by the gallery for the opening, whether the catalog is to be in black and white or color, and the kinds and extent of advertising to be done.

Agreement on these matters is important not only to determine the extent and manner of exposure to be given to the artist, but also to determine if the gallery is entitled to claim a lien for these expenses if a falling out between gallery and artist ensues. In a number of cases, galleries have attempted to retain the paintings of artists in satisfaction of their "lien" when the relationship has deteriorated. A suit by the artist to regain possession is expensive and time-consuming, and can be avoided simply by an express agreement that no lien shall result from any such outlay of money by the gallery.

Gallery's Compensation

One of the most important questions to be decided in any contract is the amount of, and method of measuring, the gallery's compensation. There are two generally employed mechanisms for measuring this, termed "net price" and "commission" methods.

In a net price arrangement, the artist gets a predetermined amount, the difference between the selling price and that amount going to the gallery. This gives the gallery wide latitude to vary price, sell several paintings for a lump sum without specifying the amount attributable to each (under a so-called "global invoice"), and otherwise to conduct freely its business, assured that its obligations to the artist are clear. It may, however, result in greater profit to the gallery than was generally contemplated if the market price for the artist's works rises, or in lessening the gallery's incentive to sell if market price falls.

A commission arrangement, where the gallery's compensation is a predetermined percentage of selling price, results in an inherently fairer split of revenue between artist and gallery, but leads to numerous problems difficult to resolve even with absolute good faith on both sides. For example, if in a specific situation the gallery deems it advisable to raise or lower a price, its duty to consult the artist and the latitude within which it may vary price without consulting the artist must be agreed upon in advance. If the gallery has wider latitude with respect to some works more than others, or makes a higher commission on some works rather than others, it may sell a group of works under a global invoice, assigning a higher than proportional value to the work that is more profitable to it. Similarly, the gallery may determine to sell a work owned by it along with one of the artist's works enhancing its own profits by assigning higher than proportional value to its own work. There are no means of assuring complete fairness under all circumstances, which is one reason that a net price arrangement is often agreed upon.

In a commission arrangement, the commission may be from 20 percent to as high as 60 percent of the sales price. Also, a sliding scale commission dependent on volume may be arranged, either to give the gallery an additional bonus for high sales volume or to provide larger rewards to the artist as his popularity grows, resulting in higher sales. The sliding scale may be on a per item basis or may be keyed to the over-all sales volume. If commissioned works are included in the agreement, a separate commission rate may be provided for them.

If more than one type of work is covered by the agreement, it may be advisable to fix different commission rates for each. For example, sculptural works require a significant investment in raw materials as compared with paintings, hence a smaller part of the sales price is compensation for the artist's work. This return on investment can be excluded from the sales price in determining commission. Although this cannot be done rigorously for each sale, if the average cost of materials is 40 percent of selling price for a given class of works, and if ordinarily the gallery's commission would be 33.3 percent, then for sculptures the gallery's commission should be only 20 percent (i.e., one-third of 60 percent). On the other hand, the artist should consider the reduction in sales incentive that might result from such a lower commission arrangement.

If the gallery is compensated on a commission basis, it may have a greater incentive to make inside sales, that is sales to itself as owner or to someone else that the gallery controls. To the extent that the gallery has latitude to lower prices, this can result in lowering the artist's compensation. If large numbers of works become owned outright by the gallery through transactions of this nature, the gallery is in a position to compete with the artist, since it is selling the artist's work both for itself and for the artist. It will naturally favor those sales that maximize its profits. Substantially the only satisfactory protection against inside sales is a net price arrangement where the incentive for such sales is removed. If, nevertheless, a commission arrangement is desired, some direct limitation upon inside sales, properly defined, may be attempted.

Records, Reports, and Payments

In many instances, galleries do not keep records in a form useful to the artist. Money may be received without an accompanying statement indicating what the payment is for. It is appropriate to require certain minimum standards of record-keeping and reporting on the part of the gallery since it is in a better position than the artist to do so.

Accurate record-keeping may be facilitated by maintaining a separate record book for each artist, a procedure that minimizes the gallery's burden of making records available for inspection by the artist. The book (or other convenient information system) should record the works received, sold, and returned to the artist, so that works in the gallery's possession may be easily identified. Preferably, a receipt should be sent to the artist for each work received by the gallery; similarly, the artist should sign a receipt for each work returned.

Provision should be made for an annual inspection of the gallery's records by the artist and for payment of any amounts due on a monthly or quarterly basis, with each payment accompanied by a brief report letter explaining the computation of the enclosed amount.

Exhibitions and instances of reproduction of any works should also be recorded and reported. Such arrangements go a long way toward making termination of the contract a less chaotic affair than it often is.

Photographs

Some galleries do a significant amount of selling through distribution of photographs of the artist's works. It may be important to the artist to have fine quality photos, or to assure that they are in color rather than black and white. It may even be important to use specific types of color film to enhance the reproduction of certain hues and tones. The artist may wish to approve all use of photographs of his work.

Generally, both parties' interests coincide to obtain excellent photographs and hence higher potential sales. But the costs of photography and the inconvenience of special arrangements fall upon the gallery, so that the artist should be willing to contribute to added costs incurred at his request or contribute to a compensatory reduction in the net proceeds payable to him.

As long as the gallery is going to have photographs made, the artist may want his own set or may want additional copies from time to time. The agreement may give the artist the right to such reproductions for a reasonable price (e.g., gallery's cost).

Advances

A gallery is often in a position to offer support to an artist, particularly early in his productive years, leaving the artist free for creative work. As payment, the gallery sometimes asks for a part of the artist's output. By this means a significant portion of the artist's output may become owned by the gallery, placing the gallery in a position to influence the market for the artist's works through sales of its own works. In competition with the artist, the gallery can no longer fairly represent him. Such an arrangement should be entered into only after carefully weighing the necessity for it and the advantage to be gained.

Illustrative of disputes that may arise because of large advances made to the artist are the extent to which an exhibit may include works of the artists owned by the gallery and how to value works for computing repayment to the gallery. Inasmuch as the gallery assumes a higher than usual risk by extending an advance, it may rightly demand repayment in works priced at a lower level than those for exhibition on behalf of the artist, or correspondingly a higher over-all commission rate.

An advance made to an artist can also give the gallery, in ensuing years, possible control over the artist's own stylistic and aesthetic development. The gallery may well contend, to the artist's dismay, that advances made in an earlier year were predicated on the continuance of the artist's early style, and that any significant change of style requires the gallery's approval. While the usual result of such a situation would be the deterioration of the relationship, hard feelings can be prevented either by avoiding advances or by an express provision in the agreement that the artist shall retain artistic and stylistic control over his output.

Pricing and Related Matters

Of central importance in any contract is the sales price of each work. An agreement may provide for prices to be determined by either the artist or the gallery alone. More often, prices are determined by joint consultation. The consequences of failure to agree on the sales price of a work should be spelled out in the agreement, for it is unlikely that lack of agreement with respect to a single work is intended to result in a termination of the relationship. For example, failure to reach agreement on the price of one work may result in giving the artist permission to sell the work on his own, with some specified commission to the gallery, at the (presumably higher) price set by the artist.

Once prices have been set, market or other conditions usually require that they be reviewed periodically and perhaps revised. How often this should be done, by whom, and within what limits, if any, are proper subjects for the contract.

The gallery should have discretionary authority to vary prices by some amount, for example 10 percent, that the parties agree to in advance. A larger leeway can be provided for sales to museums. Naturally, the parties are always free to vary the prices outside the stipulated limits by specific agreement in each instance.

If a commission basis is agreed upon, the contract may require the gallery to obtain cash payment in full for each sale, as opposed to whole or partial payment in other works or merchandise, thereby avoiding disputes over the value of such works or merchandise. Additionally, the gallery may be required to guarantee to the artist the credit of its clients. Many galleries rent paintings and, if this is contemplated, a separate commission rate should be provided for rentals, as well as a rental rate structure.

Additionally, the time should be agreed upon when payment to the artist becomes due on any given sale. The gallery may sell on time, may inadvertently accept a bad check, or may come up against other credit problems that result in failure to collect the full amount of the sale. If the gallery did not agree to guarantee the credit of the client, the gallery's responsibility in such circumstances should be clearly specified. Usually, the gallery is in a better position than the artist to judge credit, collection, and related matters, and should be given discretion to do so. The legal expenses incurred may or may not be deducted in part from the artist's payment. It may be agreed, for example, that the gallery can make whatever credit or extended payment arrangements it wishes provided that the artist's share is paid in full within six months of sale. As an alternative it may be agreed that the first monies received belong to the artist, so that the gallery bears the greater burden of non-collection with respect to its commission.

Droit de Suite: Receiving a Portion of Incremental Value

One other factor, of fairly recent interest in the United States, should be considered. Under the laws of many European countries, the artist has the so-called right of *droit de suite*, which permits him (or his estate) to share subsequently in the incremental value of his work.[3] Under this concept, if an artist at an early stage of his career sells a painting for $200 and years later the work is resold for $5,000, he would be entitled to receive a portion of the $4,800 incremental gain. This is not the law in the United States. However, in the past year a group of lawyers and artists have developed a form entitled "The Artist's Reserved Rights Transfer and Sale Agreement" by which it is proposed to grant substantially this right by *contract* to the artist.[4] The procedure contemplates that when an artist or his gallery sells a work by the artist, the purchaser, by signing the form, shall agree that a percentage (15 percent) of the appreciated value would be paid to the artist or his estate, and that the purchaser (and each subsequent purchaser) shall obtain execution of a similar form from the next purchaser of the work. The duration of the obligation is for the period of twenty-one years after the deaths of the artist and the artist's surviving spouse.

The innovative form also contemplates:

a) a record of ownership of the work at any given time;

b) the right of the artist to be notified when the work is to be exhibited, so that the artist can advise upon or veto the proposed exhibition of his work;

    c) the right of the artist to borrow the work for exhibition for two months every five years (at no cost to the owner);

    d) the right of the artist to be consulted if repairs become necessary;

    e) payment to the artist of half of any rental income paid to the owner for the exhibition of the work; and

    f) all reproduction rights in the work to be retained by the artist.

The form is a very creative document in its attempt to import certain civil law concepts into traditional American assumptions of private property and customary practices of purchasing and exchanging art. As is obvious, however, the use of this form requires the purchaser to agree to sign the form (and indeed to have his subsequent purchaser similarly sign the form) and the development of effective enforcement techniques to police the subsequent sales and payments to the artist.

The form has, moreover, been criticized as being oblivious to the "simple economics" of the proposed contract.[5] It is argued that by requiring that collectors pay 15 percent of the profit from the sale or exhibition of an art work, they are imposing a "tax" on the sale and exhibition of art. First, it is pointed out that if the collector must pay a portion of his profit to the artist, but cannot recover any part of his loss, the collector will not be willing to pay the price requested. Further, since collectors may still purchase "used" paintings and graphics without concern for the agreement, they will shift their purchasing to works not subject to the form. It is further argued that since an artist benefits by having his work sold, preferably at high prices, the movement to purchase works not restricted by the agreement will hurt the working artist. Finally, it is pointed out that collectors who wish to avoid the obligations of the form will attempt to sell art in "packages" and assign a lower value to the work subject to the form, thereby depriving the artist of his incremental value and the publicity that he would otherwise receive from having his art appreciate in value. Only time will tell if this form becomes a custom of the trade or an intriguing historical footnote.

Miscellaneous Provisions

If a gallery sells through another gallery, usually in a different locale, this may increase the total commission payable, netting somewhat less to the artist. If sold from museum exhibitions, the museum's "handling charge" may be equivalent to a sub-gallery's commission and should be similarly provided for.

In case a work is lost, through fire, theft, or other casualty beyond the party's control, separate provision should be made for division of the insurance proceeds, and the artist should request that he be designated as a named assured in the insurance policy obtained by the gallery. Provision should be made for obtaining and paying for insurance on works in shipment and in the gallery's custody. The contract may provide that the works may be insured for less than 100 percent of the proposed retail selling price. If the agreement is silent, the artist would generally bear the risk of loss due to fire, theft, or other damage beyond the reasonable control of the consignee-gallery.

If the artist is required to ship work overseas for the gallery, the impact of customs regulations must be considered. Often the artist, if he is to bear the cost of shipment, must ship the work without insurance by declaring it valueless in order to avoid paying duty. This should be clearly settled between the artist and gallery.

Responsibility for framing paintings should be determined in the agreement, as well as whether the frame price is to be included in the commission base. This may become important, as sometimes the frame may be nearly as costly as the painting.

3

THE ARTIST AND
THE PUBLISHER

TYPES OF PUBLICATION

An artist's relationship with a publishing house may take various forms. In order to comprehend fully these relationships and the reasons for them, the publisher's role must be understood. A publisher is defined as "one that issues and offers for sale books or other printed material."[1] A publisher does not in the strictest sense function as a retailer or as a printer of a particular work. The publisher has the responsibility for bringing a work before the public.

The types of relationships between an artist and his publisher vary because a publisher may have many other roles. For example, publishers also own art galleries and therefore one type of agreement may include the types of provisions covered under the chapter on the relationship between the artist and the gallery; or a publisher may be a wholesaler that publishes and distributes artwork through channels to galleries, dealers, and other retail outlets including department stores, or through the mail.[2] Many gallery-publishers also act as wholesalers. Also there are a number of print workshops in the country where it is possible for an artist to have his work printed and distributed.

There are a number of basic situations in which an artist will find himself in contact with a publisher. He may a) have an existing work of his reproduced, b) create a graphic work for reproduction and distribution as an edition, or c) provide illustrations for a book to be published.

THE AGREEMENT

Not only does the type of publisher create differences in the relationship, but also the variety of contract practices that have developed within the art world permits variations. An artist may, for example, contract with a publisher-gallery or he may contract for an exclusive agreement with a wholesaler to provide a certain number of works per year for a number of years. Remuneration may be a flat yearly fee payable monthly, or a royalty (often with an advance at the beginning of the contract and possibly at other stated intervals).

It should be noted at the outset that contracts with publishers should always be in writing. All too often what an artist may take for granted is found to be to the contrary, after his work has begun. For example, many artists are under the impression that the physical illustrations they submit under contract to a book publisher belong to them and will be returned after plates are struck and the publisher has made use of the illustrations to the extent desired.

Written contracts may range from informal one or two paragraph letter agreements to complex legal documents. The shorter letter agreements merely set forth the basic terms, such as the type of illustrations required, the consideration to be paid to the artist, the rights to be conveyed, and a warranty by the artist that his works are original. Some agreements state nothing more than that the publisher will receive "world rights" (a shorthand term that refers to all rights) in the works. If an artist has previously dealt with a publisher, he may be confident that a simple letter agreement is all that is needed, even though many of the terms and provisions are not spelled out. However, since the prior course of dealing may be difficult to prove or possibly inadmissable in evidence, such confidence may be misplaced. Usually an artist will be confronted with a "standard" printed form used by the publisher. Depending upon the artist's bargaining power, these form contracts can be changed.

The Artist's Work

The contract should clearly describe the work requirement that the artist must satisfy. For example, an illustration contract may provide for 14 drawings or illustrations in three colors, full page or half page, cover design, and so forth. A graphics contract will generally not be as specific, allowing the artist more latitude, but will provide for the method of reproduction (i.e., silk screen, lithograph, etching, etcetera), color, size of image, the size of edition, and whether and how the works are to be signed and numbered, and possibly designation of printer. A reproduction contract will designate or describe the work or works, method of reproduction, and describe the publication.

The artist generally is required to use his best efforts to create his work and to submit preliminary sketches (with or without a sample of finished work) by a certain date.[3] Some contracts may provide that delay or failure to provide preliminary sketches may result in a penalty amounting to a reduction in the fee or, in some cases, termination of the contract.[4] The agreement may also provide that the works will not be changed without the consent of the artist; but an illustration contract may provide that minor changes requested by a publisher shall be made by the artist without extra charge.

As a counterpart to the submission of preliminary sketches by the artist in a book illustration contract, a graphics contract will provide for the submission by the publisher of a print proof to be approved by the artist. This is known as *"bon a tirer,"* which means "good to print." The artist usually approves the print proof by signing his name at the bottom after which the print is returned to the printer or publisher to indicate that the edition may be run. The reproduction contract will normally provide for a similar procedure.

The contracts ordinarily provide a delivery schedule for final works, and again delay or failure to meet the schedule may result in some form of penalty. Since book illustration contracts may cover a number of years and a number of jobs there may be a number of delivery schedules. For example, a book publisher may enter into an agreement with an artist for two years during which time the artist is to supply illustrations for two or three books. The contract may set out the names of the books that the artist will work on, or a list of books from which the artist may choose, and the time schedules and specifications for each book involved for the two-year period.[5] Graphics contracts may also provide for time periods—time within which the artist is to supply his work and time within which a publisher must use his best efforts to sell the artist's works.

Rights in the Work

Some book illustration contracts provide that all right, title, and interest, including copyright and the right to the physical drawings, shall vest in the publisher, along with the sole and unrestricted right to the use of the work.[6] However, these types of contracts have been liberalized over the last few years and now it is not uncommon to find contracts that limit publishers to publication, reproduction, and promotion rights and some book club and other reprint editions; motion picture, television and other commercial rights; first serial (sale of the work or parts to newspapers and periodicals before book publication) and second serial rights (sale of the work or parts to newspapers and periodicals after book publication)—while retaining for the artist the right to have the work copyrighted in his name and the right to the physical drawings after a certain length of time.[7] As protection for the publisher, it is usually provided that there is no obligation to use illustrations submitted to it under the contract.[8]

In a graphics contract, the rights that will be conveyed to the publisher will often include production, sales, promotion, catalog, publicity, and limited publication rights. This is true of a reproduction contract also. Publication rights are usually limited to one edition of a certain number of reproductions of the artwork, and possibly an additional edition of a certain number. As for ownership of the physical work, the contract may provide for return to the artist after reproduction, and insurance of the work while it is in the hands of the publisher. In an illustration contract, the publisher ordinarily disclaims himself as an insurer.[9] Copyright is obviously more important to the graphics artist and the contract should provide for copyright in his name.

It should be borne in mind that the manufacturing requirements of the Copyright Act apply to illustrations in books and to separate prints, if produced by a lithographic or photoengraving process.[10] Thus, such printings would have to be made in the United States to protect United States copyright. However, these requirements do not apply if the "subjects represented" in the pictures "are located in a foreign country and illustrate a scientific work or reproduce a work of art." This language has been liberally construed and appears to exempt a print reproducing any art work permanently located abroad, even if the work was prepared for the express purpose of reproduction of the print.[11]

Warranty

A publication contract invariably will contain a warranty that the artist's work is original and does not infringe upon any copyright or violate any other rights and is not unlawful in any respect. In this connection, it is provided that the artist shall indemnify the publisher for damages and expenses incurred by reason of a violation of the warranties. As additional protection the publisher will often require the artist to obtain and furnish written permission to use any material reproduced in the work that has been copyrighted by someone else.[12]

Remuneration

Payment for artwork may take a number of forms. Basically an artist will be paid either on a flat fee basis or on a royalty basis. An artist contracting to do the illustrations for a book may agree to a sum that will be payable on a monthly basis.[13] He may enter into a royalty contract that will ordinarily provide him with 5 percent or less on the catalog retail price on each book sold, except for books provided free of charge, samples, damaged copies, or books sold below cost;[14] or, in the case of graphics, provide for a royalty on each print sold. Royalty contracts often provide for a semi-annual accounting by the publisher and the right of the artist to inspect the publisher's books.[15] Generally, an advance of a few hundred dollars or so may be made on royalty contracts and sometimes on flat fee contracts.

Payment provisions reached in graphics contracts are often closely associated with those provisions found in an agency relationship reached with a gallery. Both flat fee arrangements and royalties on prints sold are common for editions. Reproduction contracts may also provide for flat fee or royalty payments although it is not uncommon for only a token fee to be paid the artist since the reproduction itself in an art book, for example, is of great value to the artist. The reproduction publisher must obtain permission to reproduce the work from the party who has the copyright or the reproduction and publication rights in the work. Thus it is not always the artist who must be paid but the owner of the "right" involved, e.g., a previous publisher. If, however, the work has been previously published, but not copyrighted, it is in the public domain. Nevertheless, it is always appropriate to obtain permission to avoid confusion and disagreements at a future date.

As further consideration, a publishing contract may provide for the division of subsidiary rights income; that is, proceeds from the sales of motion picture, mechanical reproduction, newspaper, magazine, translation, dramatic, radio or television rights.[16] In some cases the artist may be apportioned 100 percent of the proceeds from the sale of a right; this is often done when there is virtually no chance of such right being sold. As an example, a book on gardening is not adaptable for motion pictures and therefore the film rights are virtually worthless. A publisher may, however, provide that proceeds from the sale of a publication right to a book club shall be shared in some proportion with the artist and this provision does have value. Finally, it is common for the artist to be presented with five or so copies of the work and be allowed a discount of 40-60 percent on additional copies that he may wish to purchase.[17]

Exclusivity

A publisher often will attempt to retain the exclusive services of the artist. A graphics publisher may, if the artist's work is sufficiently valuable, attempt to enter into an exclusive contract to publish all of the artist's work during a certain period of time. A book publisher, on the other hand, generally wishes an exclusive service clause for a negative or protective purpose; that is, to keep, in effect, the artist's other work from competing with that supplied to the publisher. Thus, an illustration contract may prohibit an artist from illustrating for another publisher books that are similar to the ones he is illustrating for the contracting publisher—i.e., travelogues, animal books, children's books—for the term of the contract.[18] Although less common, a reproduction contract may prohibit a work or series of works from being reproduced in a competing or similar publication for a certain period of time. The contract that covers the reproduction of one work of art, or a single portfolio, or the illustration of one book, will generally not contain an exclusive service clause, except in unusual circumstances.

Termination

There are a number of reasons why the parties to the publishing contract may wish to terminate the agreement. The failure of the publisher to keep the work in print or for sale, or the opinion of the publisher that the work is no longer merchantable or profitable, or the sell-out of an edition are grounds in some contracts for termination. Clearly, however, if the contract is basically an agency agreement with a gallery, the publisher has obligations to the artist to represent him to the public and termination may not be so simple. Bankruptcy, insolvency, or liquidation of the publisher are also deemed grounds for termination in many contracts.[19] In all such cases, it is generally provided that all rights originally granted by the artist to the publisher revert to him. The contract may also provide for transfer of copyrights to the artist, if he does not already have the copyrights in his name, and may give the artist the opportunity to purchase any existing plates.[20]

4

STUDIO SALES AND
COMMISSIONED WORKS

STUDIO SALES

It has been customary through the years for an artist to sell his work directly to the ultimate buyer without the intervention of a gallery or a museum. These sales, which generally were casual transactions at the artist's studio, often represented a substantial part of the artist's income.

The usual transaction involved the exchange of a painting or other work for money or its equivalent. The exchange closed the bargain. Generally, the buyer realized from the transaction all the rights to the work including the right to reproduce it.[1] The artist, usually without realizing exactly what he was transferring, granted to the buyer all right, title, and interest in the work. Thus, artworks were treated in a manner similar to other tangible personal property.[2]

More knowledgeable artists began to realize that there was a distinction between the tangible work of art and the intangible rights arising from it, and that these intangible rights also had value. Therefore, when bargaining power permitted, artists began entering into short agreements with purchasers to retain reproduction rights.[3] In 1966, New York attempted to assist the artist further by enacting a statute providing for retention of reproduction rights unless such rights are expressly transferred by writing.[4] Doubts have been expressed, however, about the scope of the statute* and the cautious artist should consider copyrighting his work and using a written agreement expressly setting forth the area of reproduction rights to be reserved.

---

*See p. 4 *supra*, and Chapter 8, p. 62. for a further discussion of the New York statute.

Aside from reproduction rights, many artists still do not enter into written agreements for these casual sales. It is important that they consider doing so and familiarize themselves with the more important provisions covered in such contracts as well as the emerging rights of artists being developed by lawyers involved in the visual arts.

Contracts for studio sales should always include a description of the work and payment terms (a flat payment, an installment arrangement, a trade, or other consideration). The delivery and payment dates should be designated and do not necessarily need to be the same. Often a later date for payment is designated, especially if the purchase price is to be in installments. If such is the case, the contract should include provisions for risk of loss and insurance coverage. Insurance and risk of loss provisions should also be included if delivery is not to be made at the artist's studio but at another location with transportation by some form of carrier. In the absence of such provisions, most state statutes provide rules specifying which party bears the risk in sales agreements.[5]

Under New York law, when a "non-merchant seller" (presumably an artist) sells a work, risk of loss passes to the buyer on receipt of notification reasonably necessary to enable the buyer to take delivery (known as "tender of delivery").[6] Thus, in the common situation where a painting is bought but left in the artist's studio to be picked up at a later date, risk of loss is on the buyer. Tender of delivery is not, however, a precise concept. In a recent New York case it was held that tender of delivery of a certain bronze sculpture, for the purpose of shifting risk of loss to the purchaser, constituted turning over the keys to certain premises and allowing a reasonable time after that for the purchaser to take physical possession.[7] In the event that a contract requires or authorizes the artist to ship a work to a particular destination, risk of loss passes to the buyer when the work is delivered to its destination.[8]

Some purchasers, especially those who buy art primarily for investment, may be concerned with obtaining a representation or warranty that the work is entirely original. Authenticity of authorship is of great importance to the collector[9] since that is the primary basis on which investment value is based.

Even with the enactment of new laws and the emerging business sophistication among artists, the artist is still cut off from his work once a sale has been made. Attempts have been, and are being made, to procure and protect for artists and their families certain future rights patterned after the civil law concept of *droit de suite*.*

COMMISSIONED WORKS

Commissioned works are works to be created by an artist in accordance with a purchaser's specifications.[10] The most typical kind of commission is for

---

*See discussion of *droit de suite* and The Artist's Reserved Rights Transfer and Sale Agreement in Chapter 2, p. 24.

a portrait. Naturally, it is even more important to enter into a written agreement for a commissioned work than it is for a casual sale of an existing work.

In addition to the provisions outlined for sales of existing works, commission agreements ordinarily specifically define the subject matter, although some patrons give the artist a great deal of leeway having chosen the artist for his style, ability, and taste. Also, the contract might include a time schedule, either required by the patron or mutually determined, covering the artist's production from preliminary sketches to finished work.

Since a commission agreement is "personal" in nature, there will ordinarily be a provision prohibiting assignment. This will prevent the artist from assigning the contract to another artist to do or complete the work and prevent the patron from assigning his part of the contract to another whose tastes, which may be entirely different, must be satisfied. Furthermore, death or serious disability of the artist before completion of the work will terminate the contract without obligation on the part of the artist or his estate. If the work is a portrait, and the subject dies prior to completion of all the sittings, the result is the same.[11]

Satisfaction is the greatest problem in a commission agreement, and a contract will normally provide, and a court will generally interpret, that the patron shall pay only if he is satisfied with the work.[12] As some measure of protection to the artist, the contract should provide for partial payments and written approvals from the patron at various stages of progress.[13] Cancellation of a commission because of dissatisfaction presents a number of problems that should be anticipated and resolved in the contract.

Ordinarily, if no partial payments have been made, the physical work and all the incidents of ownership, including copyright, belong to the artist. However, the resolution of ownership rights becomes knotty in the event the contract is silent on the point and there has been included a provision for partial payments that the artist is entitled to retain, or there has been payment of a portion of the full consideration. Therefore, the contract should specify what rights the artist and patron have on cancellation, including the right of the artist to dispose of the work. In the absence of contract language, permission is ordinarily necessary to dispose of a portrait since display may be an invasion of privacy or a form of libel.[14]

CHAPTER
5

THE ARTIST AND
THE MUSEUM

At the outset the museum* should be placed in its historical setting. A professor of art history recently suggested the focus:

> The first great art museum for the general public—the Louvre—was the creation of the first great radical upheaval of our time. In a sense, the creation of the museum was a token of art's impotence, its final severance from the social structure, setting it apart, like religion, for weekend worship. Yet, in another sense, the museum was from the start conceived of as an instrument of cultural re-integration on a higher level, a means of spreading historical and esthetic knowledge among an everbroadening segment of society, allowing to all a share of the cultural manna which had formerly been the food of a privileged few. As the shrine of an elitist religion and at the same time a utilitarian instrument for democratic education, the museum may be said to have suffered from schizophrenia from the start.[1]

The "schizophrenia" may, however, be only a function of the vantage point of the beholder. Thus, the writer continues:

> Today, for example, much depends on whether one is looking at the museum from the viewpoint of the radical (or advanced) artist, from that of the radical member of the public, or that of the radical

---

*There are various kinds of museums: public institutions, which are generally supported by governmental funds (e.g., Smithsonian Institution); private institutions, which receive a substantial portion of their income from local governments (e.g., Metropolitan Museum of Art); private institutions, which look to their own membership for support (e.g., Museum of Modern Art); and university museums (e.g., Yale University Art Gallery).

museum worker. The radical artist may, for example, want to do away with the whole concept of the museum (which he conceives of as a mortuary for dead cultural artifacts) and the whole notion of art-as-objects, calling for a merging of life and art, or the death of art. The political radical, on the contrary, may call for an art of greater social relevance and immediate comprehensibility and may sneer at non-art, anti-art, environments, concepts, software and process as simply more of the same bourgeois elitism and mystification.

The formation of art museums in the United States coincides with the rise of great industrial fortunes in the last half of the nineteenth century. Modern museums of art thus began with the patronage of the wealthy and survive in this manner in significant respect today.[2] The democratizing of museums is unquestionably relatively recent, and still evolving.[3]

The typical United States museum is privately controlled, supervised by its own board of trustees, and supported by tax-exempt endowments or gifts.[4] Because of this, the museum as such is not subject to direct state or federal regulations, and it has developed, in the areas where custom and negotiation prevail, its own criteria as to the unique role it sould play *vis-a-vis* the artist.

Some of the artist's relationships with the museum fall quite readily into certain well-defined areas of the law, such as contracts or bailments. In many situations, however, the interaction between an artist and the museum falls into an area where custom, usage, and negotiation are the governing factors. Although in many areas of contact the museum treats the artist the same as other donors of work, there are a few specific situations that are of unique concern to the artist.

RIGHT OF REPRODUCTION

As previously discussed,* the American artist seldom copyrights his work and runs the risk that, if publicly displayed, it may be freely copied or reproduced. Despite this fact, museums as a matter of courtesy generally pay royalties to an artist for reproductions made or permitted by the museum, except those made primarily for educational purposes. For similar reasons, publishers generally purchase reproduction rights before publishing the work of any living artist. If such reproduction rights are obtained by a publisher from a museum owning the artist's work, the museum frequently divides the royalties with the artist or his surviving spouse or heirs. The Whitney Museum of American Art in New York City, for example, pays the artist 50 percent of any royalties it receives for reproductions suitable for framing, or reproductions used on Christmas cards or book jackets. Royalties are usually not paid, however, for slides, post cards, or

---

*See Chapter 1.

book illustrations. If the artist refuses to consent to reproduction, the material is normally not used, even though it may be in the public domain.

Since trade custom is the controlling factor in this particular area of the artist-museum relationship, each museum has different internal rules and practices regarding the type of item on which royalties will be paid, the percentage of royalties remitted to the artist, correcting proofs, payment to surviving spouse or heirs, and the like.

In rare instances, most often when a work has been obtained from a gallery, all reproduction rights are by contract reserved to the artist. The Joint Artists-Museums Committee, a group of representatives of various museum and artists' associations, has recommended that "contemporary American artists . . . should be paid fees or royalties for . . . reproductions, except reproductions for primarily educational purposes; . . . and that all such fees or royalties should continue to be paid to the artist's heirs and assigns for ten years after his death. . . ."[5]

The New York Statute that provides that reproduction rights are reserved to artists (unless expressly granted) is generally ignored by museums, apparently because of its vagueness and possible inconsistency with the federal copyright statute.[6]

GIFTS TO A MUSEUM

One area for potential conflict between the artist and museum involves the gift of art burdened with restrictions. An artist might wish to donate one of his works to a museum, but with the stipulation that it be kept on permanent display. Since many museums have wall space for perhaps as little as 5 percent of their collection, they are naturally unwilling to so restrict themselves. Museums will sometimes accept a gift under such restrictions, but generally only from extremely prominent artists.

Another area of potential friction is the question of the disposition, whether by sale or exchange, of the work of a living American artist from a museum collection.[7] If the work has been given by the artist, he may dispute the museum's right to dispose of it, whether by sale or donation to another museum. As a legal matter, it is probable that the museum may dispose of its property in any way it chooses. The Joint Artists-Museums Committee has recommended that no such disposition be made by a museum except after consultation with the artist. Many major museums follow this policy. One currently important, and quite controversial, aspect of the problem of gifts by an artist to museums is the extent of the charitable deduction permitted to the artist. Prior to the Tax Reform Act of 1969, an artist, like most other donors, was entitled to deduct on his income tax return the market value of the gift. As a result of the Tax Reform Act, the artist (unlike most other donors who purchased the work) is restricted to the cost of his materials.*

---

*See Chapter 6, p. 42.

LOANS TO A MUSEUM

The loan of a work of art to a museum by an artist is an area in which, generally speaking, certain well-defined legal relationships apply. In the absence of a contract to the contrary, "ordinary rules of bailment would apply if a work of art were in the possession of the museum for examination or otherwise. . . ."[8] Thus, a museum is liable if it fails to exercise proper care for the work of art on loan.[9]

With respect to open exhibitions, most major museums no longer charge entry fees to artists for handling, packaging, unpacking, exhibiting, and hanging. Special conditions are usually negotiated between the artist and museum, and should be covered in detail in a loan agreement. For example, the fragility of a work may require special handling and display; in fact, a work may be so fragile that the artist may be required to assume all risk of loss or damage.

Generally speaking, the loan agreement should specify in detail the rights and responsibilities of the artist and museum. For the most part, it should specify receipt of the work, the length of the loan, describe the object, detail the precautions to be taken for the preservation and safety of the object, fix responsibility for loss or damage, specify the insurance valuation and coverage,* detail reproduction rights, provide an option to purchase (if any), restoration or repair (if required), framing (if required), catalog reproduction and publicity, and sale price if the work is to be sold. Other matters, such as obligation to exhibit and the method of installation or exhibit, may also be covered.

As a general rule, most of these terms are subject to negotiation. For example, if the museum feels the value placed on the work by the artist is too high, it may insist that a more reasonable insurance value be placed on it before agreeing to accept it for display. If the work has been on consignment with a gallery, the gallery commission is sometimes deducted from the value of the work. If the insurance carried by the artist provides adequate coverage, the museum may agree to reimburse the artist on a pro rata basis for the time the work is on loan. Special problems are created by conceptual works, in which the artist exercises only a supervisory function, and works that are industrially fabricated. At least one major museum limits its liability for such work to the cost of refabrication. If the work is sold as a result of display in the museum, the museum often receives a commission as specified in the loan agreement.

SALES TO A MUSEUM

The terms of a sale of a work by an artist to a museum are closely governed by contract. The bill of sale should include a description of the work,

---

*Most museums insure objects on loan "wall to wall"; that is, from the time it leaves the owner's possession to the time it is returned to his possession.

warranty of authorship and ownership, price, date, and similar matters. If the artist wishes to retain copyright and reproduction rights, a clause to that effect should be included in the bill of sale. If the artist is offering the object to the museum at an especially advantageous price, he may wish to retain the right of first refusal in the event the museum decides to sell the work.

RIGHT OF THE ARTIST TO CONTROL THE USE
AND DISPLAY OF HIS WORK

One of the most controversial topics in the art world in recent years has been whether the artist retains certain rights, such as the right to determine whether or not a work is suitable to a given exhibition or is properly displayed, even after legal title has passed out of his hands. The "Takis Affair" is illustrative of this controversy. On January 3, 1969, the Greek artist Takis Vassilakis removed a piece of his sculpture, which he had sold to the museum, from an exhibition at the Museum of Modern Art. With several friends, he carried the sculpture to the museum's outdoor garden and sat near it, refusing to move until permitted to confer with the museum director. The museum finally agreed to place the work in storage.[10]

Recognition of the artist's right to control the subsequent use of his work in such a fashion undoubtedly would raise a number of rather formidable problems. These might include conflicting demands made by an artist after the museum had expended a great deal of time and expense mounting a show of his works, or threats by artists to forbid the use of their works in an attempt to require political action on the part of the museum.

The right of the artist to control the later use of his work is a well defined legal concept in many civil law countries, but not in the United States. The civil law concept, developed chiefly in France and Germany, is termed *droit moral* or the moral rights of the author. Among these rights are included "the right to prevent others from making deforming changes or truncations of the work" and "the right to be known as the creator of the work."[11] Moral rights have been defined as "non-property attributes of an intellectual and moral character which give legal expression to the intimate bond which exists between literary or artistic work and its author's personality."[12]

The basic thrust of the doctrine of moral right is to protect the artist from "any use of his name or misuse of his work which would reflect discredit upon his capability and talent as an artist."[13] The doctrine protects personal rights of artists "as distinguished from their merely economic rights."[14] The artist's moral right is a long-lasting one, and has been held to extend even to paintings that were cut up and thrown away by the artist and later sold by another party into whose possession they had come.[15] The moral right has been extended even to a refrigerator decorated by the painter Bernard Buffet.[16] It should be noted that in countries that recognize the *droit moral*, the right does not permit the artist to control the form or manner of the museum's exhibition, if no deforming changes are made in the work or if the exhibition does not reflect on the artist's professional standing.

Numerous authors have pointed out American analogues to the *droit moral*, but these are much more limited than the Continental version. One author states that "private legislation in the form of contract gives the best assurance that an [artist] can obtain against the use of his work by another in a way he finds offensive."[17]

It should be pointed out finally, that, at least in New York, an artist who seeks to interfere physically with the display of his work in a museum risks criminal penalties. New York law provides that "whoever intentionally injures, defaces or destroys any property belonging to *or deposited in* any . . . museum . . . shall be punished by imprisonment in a state prison for not more than three years . . . or by a fine of not more than $500.00, or by both. . . ."[18] (Emphasis supplied.) While it is unlikely that such penalties would be applied in the absence of serious misconduct, the artist genuinely concerned with the proper display of his works is well advised to provide for such display by agreement with the museum, rather than resorting to private remedies.

MEDIATION AND ARBITRATION

It has been suggested that boards of mediation and arbitration be established to help solve disputes between artists and their patrons, galleries, or museums.[19] A board might consist of members of the art world or might be provided by the American Arbitration Association.

Mediation is a process by which "a third party may be asked to lend his good offices to help solve the problem," but which "in no way binds the respective parties."[20] Arbitration, on the other hand, takes place according to an agreement, is binding on the parties involved, and often uses the services of an arbitrator who is an expert in the field of dispute.

The establishment of "artists' courts" or widely accepted arbitration procedures would have a profound effect not only on the relationship presently existing between the artist and the museum, but undoubtedly would affect a host of other ancillary relationships relating to the museum and its functional role in the community that it serves.

CHAPTER

6

TAX PROBLEMS
OF THE ARTIST

Artists, just as other people, are subject to taxes. This chapter deals with the effect three federal taxes—income tax, gift tax, and estate tax—have on artists. It by no means attempts to deal with all of the tax problems of artists. State and city tax questions (such as the applicability of the amended New York City unincorporated business tax[1]), excise tax questions, and individual tax problems faced by each artist are left for consultation between the artist and his own tax counsel.

INCOME TAX

Of all federal taxes affecting an artist, the tax having the greatest day-to-day effect is the income tax, and each artist should have a basic understanding of the way his income is treated.

Treatment of Income

Income may be realized by an artist in one of two ways: either from the sale of his works, or as fees, salary, wages, or commissions paid for his services (for example, in painting a mural under contract, or as a result of employment by a publisher). When an artist performs services, he is treated as are other professionals or employees who perform services, and his compensation is regarded as "ordinary income,"[2] which is taxed under a progressive rate schedule that increases with the amount of income earned (subject to a number of exemptions, exclusions, and deductions).[3] When an artist sells his works, he is engaging in business, and the price he receives for all of his sales in one year, less the cost of his raw materials and his regular business expenses (such as the cost of operating his studio) is his ordinary income for the year.[4]

Basically, the tax treatment of art dealers is the same, except that instead of deducting the cost of raw materials from his sales price, the art dealer deducts the purchase price that he paid for the artists' works and other business expenses such as rent and advertising. Since artists and art dealers are both engaged in the business of selling, their profits are ordinary income.

A collector, on the other hand, is treated differently from an artist or a dealer. He is not in the business of selling art; he is an investor. As such, he may receive more favorable treatment on the profits he realizes from work that he purchases, holds for investment, and later sells. Because he has not created the work and is not holding it for "sale in the ordinary course of business to customers," the works he acquires are deemed "capital assets." When he sells them, his profits are treated as "capital gains."[5] If the capital gains result from the disposition of property held (or treated as held) for more than six months they may be treated in a manner that effectively taxes them at one-half the rates at which ordinary income is taxed.[6]

The income recognized by artists and dealers from art sales is not capital gains because the sales are made in the ordinary course of business.[7] However, if an artist or gallery purchases art to collect and holds it for investment, profits realized upon its sale may be treated as capital gain. It may be difficult for a dealer to convince the Internal Revenue Service that a particular work is held for investment since he is always buying and selling, but an artist, if he does not normally deal in other artists' works, should not have the same difficulty.

Other Dispositions Resulting in Income

Sometimes an artist does not sell his work in the usual manner. Different dispositions may or may not change the income tax effect. For example, if an artist exchanges his works with other artists, those exchanges will be treated as sales.[8] Accordingly, the artist will be treated as having received income equal to the value of the work he receives less his cost of the raw materials for the work he delivers.[9] Determining the value of the property the artist receives is a problem that shall be discussed later in this chapter.

If an artist assigns his copyright in a work (perhaps to permit reproduction of the work in a publication, for example), the compensation he receives— whether it is paid in one lump sum or over a period of time, and whether it is measured by sales of reproductions or is a fixed amount—is ordinary income.[10] Generally, even if the contract of purchase of the copyright specifies the exact amount the artist is to receive over the full period of time during which the purchaser may use the copyrighted material (rather than having payment determined by the sales of reproductions), the artist will not be taxed until the income is paid to him each year and then only upon the amount he receives in that particular year.[11]

Provisions of Law that Reduce Tax Burdens

An artist's income may fluctuate substantially from year to year based upon his productivity and the marketability of his works. Because the federal income tax rates are progressive as the amount of income in any one year grows larger, it would be useful if an artist could treat the income he receives in a boom year as having been received over a period of lean years. Fortunately, the federal income tax laws provide a method for such averaging. If an individual's income exceeds 120 percent of his average income of the prior four years (and that excess is at least $3000), he will usually find it advantageous to treat that excess as if it had been received in equal amounts in the current year and the preceding four years. The advantages of income averaging benefit the artist whose income increases sharply after a period of three or four lean years, but depending upon the actual fluctuations, the advantages may continue after that for two or three years, or even indefinitely if his income continues to accelerate sharply. The computation of the effective tax rate upon the average-able income spread over the five-year period is fairly involved and goes beyond the scope here. Accordingly, if the artist thinks he may qualify to use this averaging method, he should consult tax counsel.[12]

Once an artist has become successful,[13] income averaging may no longer be useful (or available) to him and his tax rate may be very high (over 50 percent). In such a case, if he does not average his income, he may be able to take advantage of the "50 percent maximum tax rate on earned income."[14] Essentially, the maximum tax rate that an artist will be required to pay upon his net earnings from the sale of his work or from salary or other payments for services will be 50 percent. (Income from other sources, such as dividends, rents, interest or gains from sales of investments, does not qualify for the 50 percent limitation; the actual computation is complicated and an artist who expects to pay a tax rate in excess of 50 percent should consult tax counsel.)[15]

Under the federal tax laws, a self-employed artist may establish a pension plan.[16] This permits the artist to set aside up to $2,500 or 10 percent of his yearly income, whichever is less, and deduct that amount in computing his tax-able income.[17] The money set aside must in general be placed in a trust with a bank to invest or in certain other special types of investments, and, until termination of the plan or distribution of the money by the trust, the earnings upon the money set aside in trust will be tax free.[18] Upon distribution of the money in the trust to the artist, he will be subject to income tax.[19] However, in order to qualify, the plan cannot in general permit any withdrawals for any reason except disability until the plan beneficiary reaches age 59½. If, upon distribution, all of the money from the pension plan is distributed in one year, the recipient has the opportunity to treat the income as if received over a five-year period.[20]

In making contributions to the trust, the 10 percent or $2,500 limitation applies to "earned income" only. Income received by the artist for the sale of his works is included in earned income, but income received through outside investments is not.[21] This is also a complicated area, and artists considering personal pension plans should obtain professional help.

Special Deductions

As stated, an artist may deduct his raw material costs from the price he receives for his works, as well as other business expenses, such as studio rent and entertainment of prospective purchasers, in computing his taxable income. There are other deductions that reduce taxable income, some discussed below.

While it may not be an ordinary occurrence, occasionally an artist may suffer a loss of his works through theft or casualty, i.e., fire, water damage, etcetera. The "cost" of each loss is deductible from his income. For this purpose, the cost of such loss equals the cost of the raw materials that have gone into the particular work.[22] The value of the artist's services in producing the work is given no credit in determining the cost for purposes of calculating the deduction.

If the artist is able to insure his works against such losses, then to the extent that the insurance proceeds exceed his costs for the raw materials, that excess will be included in his income.[23] Essentially, the insurance proceeds are treated the same as the price paid by a customer for the lost, stolen, or destroyed work. The cost of the insurance premium is deductible by the artist as an ordinary and necessary business expense.[24]

Another deduction from income may be obtained by an artist through gifts to charity or to a museum. While no deduction is available in connection with an ordinary gift, if a gift is made to a charity or a museum, the artist will be permitted to take a charitable deduction.[25] Since the enactment of the Tax Reform Act of 1969, the amount of the deduction available for each artwork given charitable organizations by the artist who created it is limited to his expenses for the raw materials.[26] This might not be the case if the artist were making a charitable contribution of a work that he had purchased from someone else. If a work is purchased by an artist for investment and not for sale in the ordinary course of business, is held for more than six months, and is then given to a museum, the charitable deduction would, in most cases, be equal to the value of the object.[27] It is interesting to note that if an artwork is retained by the artist who created it and donated to a museum *by his estate*, the charitable deduction will be equal to the value of the work and not merely the artist's costs in creating it. Thus, an artist has incentive to retain his works and let his family donate them to charity after his death rather than donating them himself.[28]

There are limitations on the total charitable deductions available to any individual in a particular year, but a discussion of those limitations is outside the scope of this monograph.[29] Suffice it to say that it is unlikely that an artist giving only his own works to charity will exceed that limitation. However, if the artist makes other charitable gifts, including money or works that he has purchased, he should seek the advice of tax counsel before making the gifts to insure that he will receive the full advantage of the potential charitable deductions.

ESTATE AND GIFT TAXES

Gift Taxes

In addition to income taxes, each artist faces problems related to gift taxes and estate taxes. Except under unusual circumstances, if a gift is made either to a private individual or a charity, the artist will not be deemed to have received any income,[30] but if the gift is not to a charity he may be required to pay a gift tax.[31]

Gift tax is paid upon the total value of "taxable gifts" made. It should be noted that the value is the work's fair market value and not merely the cost of the raw materials, and it is upon this value that the tax must be paid. In computing taxable gifts made, an artist may exclude in each taxable year all gifts made to any person, if the value of the gifts made to that person in such year does not exceed $3,000. Thus, in any one taxable year, an artist may give gifts totalling $3,000 to his son, $3,000 to his daughter, and $3,000 to each one of his friends or other relatives without any of those gifts being considered taxable. If the artist is married, by having his spouse join him in making a gift (even though the work is produced only by the artist), he may raise the amount of the tax-free gifts to each separate person per year to $6,000.[32]

Also, the artist has a total lifetime exemption of $30,000 worth of otherwise taxable gifts that he may give without paying tax.[33] Even if his gifts to each person in a year exceed $3,000 (or $6,000 if the artist's spouse joins him in making the gifts), the gifts may still not be taxable if the value of all gifts made at any time in his life in excess of the $3,000 (or $6,000) yearly exclusion applicable to each recipient do not add up to $30,000.

If the artist is married, then his spouse's unused lifetime exemption may be used with respect to up to one-half of his gifts to persons other than his spouse, so that as much as $60,000, rather than $30,000, of otherwise taxable gifts will be exempt.[34]

The following example may illustrate the use of the lifetime exemption: Artist A, who is not married, gives his mother B a gift in 1971 valued at $5,000. After deducting the yearly $3,000 exclusion, A will have a $2,000 taxable gift unless he has not used up his lifetime exemption of $30,000. If A has never used his lifetime exemption and elects to do so, the entire gift to B is tax free, but A's lifetime exemption is reduced to $28,000. In 1972, A gives B a gift valued at $32,000. After subtracting the $3,000 annual exclusion, the taxable gift would be $29,000, but if A elects to use his lifetime exemption (which is now reduced to $28,000) the taxable gift is reduced to $1,000.

Once the yearly per-person exclusions and the lifetime exemption are used up by the artist, he will be taxed upon the fair market value for all gifts that he makes. The gift tax rates become progressively higher as the total of all taxable gifts increases. For example, if the artist makes a taxable gift of $5,000 in one year, he will pay a tax upon $5,000. If three years later he makes a second taxable gift of $5,000, the tax rate will be upon $10,000, but there will be a credit for the tax previously paid on the first $5,000 gift.[35] Thus, the rate of tax paid becomes higher and higher throughout the life of the artist, depending on the total value of all taxable gifts he has made, and is not determined only by the size of the particular gift.

It may be of interest to the artist to know that if he makes a gift of a work and the work is later sold by the recipient of the gift (the "donee"), the donee will recognize ordinary income upon the sale of the work based on the sale price, less the artist's cost of the raw materials (subject to certain adjustments). Despite the fact that the donee may not be in the business of selling art and may have held the work that he received by gift as an investment, the federal tax law provides that the donee of an artist is not permitted to treat the artwork as a "capital asset" and will not receive capital gains upon its sale.[36]

Estate Taxes

At the death of an artist, his estate will be taxed upon the value of the property he owns, less certain deductions.[37] The use of the word "owns" in this case is not precise. The federal estate tax laws treat various kinds of powers possessed by the deceased with respect to property as ownership of such property, and include such property as "owned" in his estate for tax purposes.[38] In some cases, this "ownership" may involve only the right to dispose of property that is owned by someone else and nothing more.[39]

Estate taxes are based upon the fair market value of the property owned, and the property value is determined at the death of the artist or at an alternate valuation date within six months after his death.[40] As with gift taxes, estate taxes are paid on the fair market value of an artist's property, including art works, and not merely on the cost of the materials that went into them. However, unlike the recipient of a gift, one who receives an artwork as a beneficiary of an artist's estate and then sells the work will have a profit measured by the excess of his sales price over the value of the work at the time of the artist's death (or the alternate valuation date); the difference between such value and the mere cost of materials will not ever be subject to income taxation. The artist may reduce his potential estate tax by leaving property to his spouse. If he is married and at his death leaves property to his widow (or through the application of the federal estate tax laws he is deemed to have left property to his widow) the value of the property that his widow receives from him (not in excess of one-half of his "adjusted gross estate") is deemed a "marital deduction" and is subtracted from the total value of his estate in computing his estate tax.[41] The precise computations of "adjusted gross estate" and "marital deduction" can be complicated. Such computations and a number of other deductions that the estate may use to reduce its tax burden are beyond the scope of this monograph.

VALUATION

It is apparent from the discussion of exchanges between artists, of gift tax, and of estate tax that the determination of the "fair market value" of artistic property may have substantial ramifications in determining taxes to be paid. Fair market value has been defined as "the price at which the property would change hands between a willing buyer, and a willing seller, neither being under any compulsion to buy or sell and both having reasonable knowledge of relevant facts."[42]

The determination of fair market value will always be a question of fact.[43] If at the time in question the works of a particular artist are uniformly selling for a particular price or within a range of prices, that price or price range will be very material in determining the fair market value of the particular work. Artworks, of course, are subject to very great changes in value from time to time.

If an artist makes a gift of his own work, it would be wise for him to retain evidence of the prices at which he is selling similar works of art to unrelated parties at the time of the gift in order to defend his evaluation of the gift for gift tax purposes. If an artist exchanges his work with another artist, he should take into consideration the sales price of the other artist's works as well as the sales price of his own in computing the amount of income that he has received for his work. Ostensibly, since the artists are willing to exchange works with each other, it could be argued that their works are equivalent in value. However, if one of the artists has been selling his work more frequently than the other, or his prices have been more stable, those factors may weigh more heavily in determining the fair market value of each of their works.

Generally, where sizeable gifts are concerned, taxpayers have relied upon appraisals from art dealers and other experts. If a substantial gift or exchange is involved the artist might also be wise in seeking an appraisal. On occasions, the Internal Revenue Service and the courts will accept appraisals if they are convinced that the appraisals are arm's-length and that the appraiser has some expertise.[44] Upon the death of an artist, an appraisal may even be required by law to support the computation of estate taxes made for his estate.[45]

The Internal Revenue Service has its own advisory panel with respect to art valuation. The panel consists of art dealers, museum curators, and art academicians who meet periodically in Washington, D.C., to advise the IRS on substantial art valuation questions with respect to whether the valuations are justified, questionable, or unjustified.[46]

ESTATE PLANNING AND SOCIAL SECURITY

There are a number of other areas related to taxation that are of vital interest to an artist. Two of these involve estate planning and social security.

Almost everyone will agree that every person should execute a Will to dispose of his estate. The failure to do so can be very costly for the estate of an artist and can deprive him of the opportunity to choose, or to control to some extent, the disposition of his unsold works and other property after his death.[47]

It is impossible here to explain in detail all of the various reasons for executing a Will. Failure to do so may result in the artist's estate paying higher estate taxes because the full marital deduction is not used. In addition, without a Will the powers that his administrators may have in handling his estate will be limited to those provided by law instead of the more extensive ones that the artist could have given to his executors. Artists Equity Association of New York, Inc., has recently published a booklet written by Emanuel Redfield of the New York Bar that examines the subject in some detail and is available to artists from that organization.

Social security is, of course, not only related to taxation but actually involves taxation. Each artist who is self-employed is required to pay a self-employment tax on his self-employment income up to $9,000 (under present law) in lieu of the social security tax paid by an employee, but the self-employment income subject to the tax is reduced by any salary received during the calendar year.[48] As a result, upon reaching the age provided by law for the payment of social security benefits, the artist may receive benefits similar to those received by an employee. Under current social security law, full benefits can be obtained upon retirement at age 65 and partial benefits upon retirement at age 62,[49] assuming in both cases that the person retiring otherwise qualifies under the law.[50]

Under current social security, upon retirement (either at age 62, 65 or earlier disability), until age 72, an artist may earn up to $1,680 per year before having any of his earnings deducted from social security benefits. Thereafter, 50 percent of the difference between $1,680 and $2,880 per year of earnings (including earnings from the sale of works) and 100 percent of his earnings in excess of $2,880 will be deducted from the amount of benefits received by the artist from social security.[51] After age 72, no deductions are made and an artist may have any income without loss of social security benefits.[52]

If an artist has questions about social security he may obtain detailed answers from any local office of the Department of Health, Education, and Welfare or he should consult counsel.

7

CONTENT AND STRUCTURE
OF ART WORKS

The right of an artist to express his ideas freely is guaranteed by the First Amendment to the United States Constitution. The right is not without bounds, however, and the content and structure of art objects created by an artist to express his ideas may be subject to legal sanctions. For example, criminal penalties may be imposed for a work that is obscene or desecrates the American flag, and an individual may sue an artist for damages for exhibiting a work ridiculing his reputation or amounting to an invasion of his privacy.

CONSTITUTIONAL RIGHTS OF ARTISTS

The First Amendment prohibits the enactment or enforcement of any law "abridging the freedom of speech, or of the press."[1] Despite the use of the words "speech" and "press" and not the general term "expression," it is generally true that other kinds of expression are also protected. The Supreme Court has held that the First Amendment protects forms of political expression, such as conducting a political demonstration,[2] carrying a red flag as a political protest,[3] and wearing a black armband in protest against the war in Vietnam.[4] In addition, nonpolitical forms of expression with aesthetic value, such as books[5] and motion pictures,[6] are protected. There is little doubt that art objects are in the category of protected forms of expression. On the other hand, "conduct" has been treated differently than "speech," even when the conduct is intended to be a form of communication. The extent to which art objects are akin to pure speech or to conduct with speech elements is uncertain.

Even if a work of art is akin to pure speech, as some courts have held,[7] the First Amendment would not grant an artist license to explore every subject matter that may appeal to him. Traditional exceptions include obscenity, libel, and so-called "fighting" words, or words which in themselves tend to cause a breach of the peace.[8] The distinctions between protected expression and these and other recognized exceptions to the First Amendment are discussed later in this chapter.

If the exhibiting of art objects is a form of conduct with speech elements,[9] then in addition to the exclusions noted other incidental limitations may be imposed where there is a sufficiently important governmental interest in regulating the "nonspeech element" in such conduct.[10] Where there is more than one way to express ideas through conduct, a form not directly conflicting with a statute should be adopted if available. Abstract or subtle artistic works are more likely to be accepted as protected conduct with speech elements than are realistic representations of the same idea.

In exhibiting works of art that may be controversial legally, it is important to provide every opportunity for people who may be offended to avoid seeing them and to leave the exhibition place at any time.[11] Where provocative nude or arguably obscene art works are exhibited, children should ordinarily be excluded or required to be with an adult.[12]

The motivation or thought process behind the creation of a work of art is irrelevant in determining whether or not it is protected by the First Amendment. First Amendment protection may not be denied merely because the ideas conveyed are controversial or unpopular, or are directed to a potentially hostile audience.[13] In fact, mere entertainment, without an intention to convey any ideas in particular, may also be protected.[14] An artist need not ignore the profit motive to maintain his constitutional rights, since First Amendment protection will not be denied merely because a form of expression is commercially motiviated.[15]

PROCEDURAL SAFEGUARDS REQUIRED BY THE FIRST AMENDMENT

Because First Amendment rights are particularly susceptible to intimidation if heavy handed methods of law enforcement are employed, certain procedural safeguards have been established to protect forms of expression that arguably are protected. While these procedural safeguards have been developed mainly in obscenity cases, there can be little doubt that other forms of expression under the First Amendment are protected as well.[16]

First and most importantly, prior to the seizure or confiscation of exhibited works of art, an adversary hearing must be held and notice must be given to the persons in charge of the works or their exhibition, and an independent determination must be made by a judicial officer that the works of art may not lawfully be exhibited or possessed for exhibition.[17] This determination must be based on a firsthand review by the judicial officer of all relevant circumstances of the exhibit, including the types of works on view, their setting and arrangement, and any precautions taken to limit the audience.[18] Hearsay statements of police officers or others are not enough, and often the only meaningful way for a judicial officer to make his determination is for him to attend the exhibit in person. If these prerequisites have not been carried out, seizure or confiscation of the works would be unconstitutional. An element of the adversary hearing is that the artist or owner of the works of art and other directly interested persons will be given an opportunity to be heard on whether the exhibition is illegal. As a practical matter, therefore, if constitutional procedures are followed by law enforcement authorities, there will be enough time for an artist and others to secure an attorney to represent their interests at the adversary hearing and prior to any seizure of art works or the closing of the exhibition.

Second, although it may be of little consolation to a professional artist, works of art held for one's own use and not for sale or exhibition cannot be seized under any circumstances. Mere private possession of such works, whether protected by the First Amendment or not, cannot constitutionally be made a crime.[19]

Regrettably, though these safeguards are meant to put the burden upon local officials to show why the status quo should be disturbed, they are often disregarded by local law enforcement officials. Since constitutional rights may be waived by explicit or implied consent, it is important to raise the procedural constitutional rights discussed here at the time they are infringed.

If the police are at the door to seize works of art without prior warning and without an adversary hearing, their actions may be protested from the outset on the grounds of the First Amendment. The fact that the police may have a search warrant does not excuse the absence of a prior adversary hearing since a search warrant is normally issued by a magistrate without notice or an adversary hearing. If a constitutional objection is to be made, it would be appropriate for the artist or anyone else in charge of the exhibit to request the officers to take official note of his protest for the police report. In addition, careful attention to procedure would dictate that the police officers be advised that their conduct constitutes infringement of constitutional rights and may result in personal liability for damages.[20] The police should not, however, be physically resisted. To resist them may be a crime even if their entrance is unjustified, and may jeopardize a civil action that might otherwise be brought later against the police.

FLAG DESECRATION

For those artists and others engaged in political protest, the use of the American flag has become a focal point for assertion of First Amendment rights. Statutes prohibiting desecration of the flag have been enacted by the federal government and virtually every state.[21] These statutes have been broadly drafted and in applying them law enforcement officers have often overlooked literal violations of the statutes by "patriotic" groups while enforcing the statutes against political protestors.[22] In a few cases, flag art has been the subject of prosecution under such statutes.[23] As yet, however, the scope of flag desecration statutes has not been satisfactorily defined, nor has there been a satisfactory judicial determination of the constitutional rights of artists to create and exhibit flag art.

Flag desecration statutes typically contain provisions making it a crime either to "cast contempt upon" the American flag or to mutilate, deface or burn a flag.[24] Examples of conduct prohibited under these statutes include the public exhibition of artistic constructions containing flags in the forms of a phallic symbol, a cannon and a body hung in effigy,[25] waving a flag wrapped around a finger at a demonstration,[26] and driving an automobile painted with a flag.[27] As a general rule, the more stark and unconventional the use of the flag the more likely it is to be considered contemptuous of the flag. A subtle abstract representation of the flag or a painting with a conventional flag and coffin motif would be less likely to be prosecuted than a flag in an obscene form.

The extent to which flag art constitutes protected expression is uncertain. Undoubtedly an attempt will be made to balance competing interests in defining First Amendment rights of flag use.[28]

The interest of the government in preserving the flag as a national symbol and of individuals in attaching personal, sometimes derogatory, significance to the flag have produced different results among lower courts in this country. Some courts have held that a statute prohibiting the casting of contempt upon the American flag is unconstitutional because such a broad prohibition would inhibit many forms of expression, such as a clenched-fist salute, which are clearly protected speech under the First Amendment.[29] Other courts have upheld such statutes as reasonable measures designed to prevent breaches of peace,[30] or to protect our national emblem as an element of national sovereignty.[31] Courts upholding these statutes suggest that whatever First Amendment rights are infringed are minimal and that alternate means not prohibited involving desecration of the flag may be adopted to express the same ideas. As a result of these conflicting interpretations and the absence of a definitive Supreme Court ruling on nonverbal communication, local situations will differ and must be examined separately.

Unique to the flag desecration statutes of New York and a few other states is a provision prohibiting the placing of any symbol or writing upon the flag.[32] This provision has been held to be unconstitutional in a recent federal court of appeals decision.[33] The court held that the peace symbol superimposed on the American flag and used as a form of political protest is protected under the First Amendment. Were it not for this decision, the exhibition of Jasper Johns' flag-on-flag constructions would undoubtedly be outlawed, as well as any number of traditional political campaign buttons and posters.

Most flag desecration statutes are so broad and vague that they prohibit many uses of the flag that have long been considered permissible. If such statutes are permitted to stand without limitation by the judiciary or the legislature, many forms of fruitful artistic expression may be stifled.

OBSCENITY

An artist may seldom give a second thought to whether his works of art are obscene or not. To him, the concept of obscenity represents a community-imposed value created by fear of the unknown or puritanical reaction to commercialism in sex.

But the fact remains that there are a myriad of criminal obscenity statutes passed by virtually every state and the federal government. A wide range of activities are prohibited, including the mailing,[34] importation through customs,[35] sale or distribution,[36] exhibition or possession for sale or exhibition[37] of obscene materials. Such restrictions have been justified on the grounds that implicit in the history of the First Amendment is a rejection of obscenity as utterly without redeeming social importance.[38]

The Supreme Court has held on First Amendment grounds that materials may not be banned as obscene unless the following test has been met:

> Three elements must coalesce: it must be established that (a) the dominant theme of the material taken as a whole appeals to the prurient interest in sex; (b) the material is patently offensive because it affronts contemporary community standards relating to the description or representation of sexual matters; and (c) the material is utterly without social value.[39]

The substance of this test has now been adopted by the New York legislature to define the word "obscene" in its statute.[40] The obscenity statutes of other states are also likely to be extended by construction or amendment to the limits permitted by the Constitution.

Increasingly greater emphasis is being placed upon the way in which sexually-oriented materials are exhibited or distributed. The First Amendment may not protect the exhibition and distribution of such art works if they are "pandered," or advertised or displayed in a manner that emphasizes only the sexual aspects of the works.[41] In the *Eros* magazine case,[42] the choice of mailing addresses with sexual connotations became an important factor in determining that the distribution of the magazine could constitutionally be prohibited. Where there is a basis for finding pandering, courts may be quick to view the artistic aspects of the works as a sham.[43]

Another factor in determining whether an exhibition of sexually provocative art may be constitutionally prohibited is the accessibility of the exhibition to minors. Some states prohibit the sale to minors of sexually provocative materials even though they may not amount to pornography, and such prohibitions have been upheld under the First Amendment.[44] In New York, it is a crime to sell or loan to a minor any art object depicting nudity, sexual conduct, or sado-masochistic abuse.[45]

A great many works escape being judged obscene because their salacious connotations must be pondered in order to be appreciated. Even works of art treating sexual subjects vividly will probably be protected under the Constitution if they represent a genuine attempt to express artistic feeling and the promotional material used in connection with their exhibition shows a sincerity of purpose.[46] Regardless of these factors, however, if works of art are meant for minors or are likely to be viewed or purchased by them, those depicting explicit sexual scenes should be excluded.

DEFAMATION AND RIGHTS OF PRIVACY

The exhibition of art objects is also subject to certain private rights of action that individuals may bring to protect their reputations and privacy. Libel, or defamation by publication, and the right of privacy are similar in nature and tend to have a much less serious impact on artistic freedom than either flag desecration or obscenity laws. Both actions are primarily private, but recovery in any case may not be granted if to do so would stifle expression protected by the First Amendment.[47]

An artist or a gallery owner or other person exhibiting a work of art may be held liable for damages caused to the professional or personal reputation of an individual or reasonably small groups of individuals who are falsely depicted in such a work of art in a derogatory pose or in a manner calculated to cause them to be ridiculed. Typical ways in which individuals might be libeled by a work of art include depicting an unnatural or obscene bodily deformity,[48] imputing nonprofessional or criminal conduct,[49] or imputing through a setting or the surrounding circumstances a lack of intelligence or manners.[50] Individuals whose reputations are damaged need not be named in the work of art. It is enough that the individuals at whom the work of art is directed are sufficiently identified to at least some of the viewers,[51] and that the number of individuals libeled is sufficiently small that the reputation of each is affected directly.[52] Honore Daumier's prints depicting courtroom scenes would thus not constitute libel since they are directed to judges and lawyers in general and not at any identifiable individuals.

Actions for violation of the right to privacy have been recognized by virtually every state.[53] Under such actions an injunction or damages may be obtained based upon the use of the name or likeness of a living person in trade or business without his permission. In four of these states (including New York), such action may also constitute a crime.[54] There is some dispute as to whether works of art may be a basis for an action for invasion of privacy. One case has held that a serious work of art cannot constitute a "portrait or picture" under the New York right of privacy statute.[55] As the court in that case stated:

[T]he figure is not more than a part of an artist's idealized conception of the pictured group in the setting which was to be his creative work. Plaintiff was only a figure in a preliminary form used as a pattern from which the artist executed his ultimate design. Such part as he found available he used. Such improvements in physique or features as he conceived desirable he adapted in the course of his work. The result cannot be regarded as a portrait or picture of plaintiff within the meaning of the Civil Rights Law [of New York].[56]

Other courts in New York have taken the view that all types of visual art objects are covered by the statute.[57] Even assuming a work of art may be the subject of a right of privacy action, the mere exhibition of a work of art containing the likeness of a living person is not enough to result in liability for invasion of privacy. Only if the work of art is used to embellish a product or in some other promotional manner beyond the customary uses of art works will an action be sustained.[58]

In preparing programmes for art exhibits, care should be taken to see that persons whose names are mentioned in a private capacity have given their consent to such use. Among those to be listed who should be asked permission are private benefactors and persons whose private collections contain the works of the artist being exhibited.

Many works of art may be protected against actions for libel or invasion of privacy on the grounds that they are fair comment or fair criticism of matters of public concern.[59] The privilege of fair comment applies to comments made upon public officials or public figures, as well as to private individuals with respect to matters of public concern. Undoubtedly Warhol's *Jackie* would be privileged on these grounds, since it presents multiple copies of a newspaper picture that most reviewers have seen many times before. The privilege may be lost, however, if the work of art is created out of malice or with a lack of regard for making a comment that is fair.[60]

Libel and the right of privacy may also be used affirmatively by artists to protect their reputation and livelihood. An artist may maintain a libel action for damage to his reputation by a public official who states that a painting is obscene.[61] Similarly, a suit may be maintained on the basis of other comments reflecting on the character of an artist. On the other hand, fair comment by a critic on the failure or lack of artistic merit of a work of art exhibited publicly is not prohibited.[62] Nor is it libelous to reproduce a work of art alone or in connection with an article provided that it is not done maliciously for the purpose of ridiculing the artist's reputation.

Under certain circumstances, a right of privacy action may be used by an artist to protect against vulgarization of his reputation. Where works of art and the artist's name are used without his permission as a promotion for the sale of products, such as a pattern for embroidered cloth, the artist is entitled to recover in damages for invasion of privacy.[63] In some states, use for trade or advertising is an essential part of an invasion of privacy action. Thus, mere reproduction of a work of art coupled with the use of the artist's name, even if included in an artistic or literary magazine sold for profit, would not be an invasion of privacy since it does not amount to use for advertising or trade.[64] The sale of a work of art will normally carry with it the right to use the artist's name at least in connection with its resale.[65]

CHAPTER

8

MISCELLANEOUS LEGISLATION IN THE FIELD

There are a number of statutes, most recently enacted, that have relevance to the work of the visual artist. These concern the art collector, gallery and the visual artist.

CALIFORNIA PRINT STATUTE

In 1970, California enacted the so-called "Print Bill," which was patterned after a proposal initially introduced in the New York State Legislature but which did not pass. This statute,[1] which is limited to "fine prints" (printed after July 1, 1971), provides that:

> No catalogue, prospectus or circular offering fine prints for sale in this state shall be knowingly published or distributed, or both, unless it clearly and conspicuously discloses the relevant informational details concerning each edition of such prints so offered. . . .

The statute is somewhat burdensome in that it further provides that no fine print shall be knowingly offered for sale, at wholesale or at retail, unless a written invoice or receipt for the purchase price or a certificate furnished to the purchaser clearly and conspicuously discloses all of the relevant informational details. If the print is described as a "reproduction," there is no need to furnish further details unless it was allegedly published in a signed, numbered, or limited edition, in which case all details are required to be furnished.

The "informational details" that are required are:

a) The name of the artist and the year when printed.

b) Exclusive of trial proofs, whether the edition is being offered as a limited edition, and, if so:

   1) The authorized maximum number of signed or numbered impressions, or both, in the edition.

   2) The authorized maximum number of unsigned or unnumbered impressions, or both, in the edition.

   3) The authorized maximum number of artist's, publisher's, printer's or other proofs, if any, outside of the regular edition; and

   4) The total size of the edition.

c) Whether the plate has been destroyed, effaced, altered, defaced or canceled after the current edition.

d) If there were any prior states of the same impression, the total number of states and a designation of the state to which the subject print relates.

e) If there were any prior or later editions from the same plate, the series number of the subject edition and the total size of all other editions.

f) Whether the edition is a posthumous edition or restrike and, if so, whether the plate has been reworked.

g) The name of the workshop, if any, where the edition was printed.

The statute further provides that a person (which would include the artist) who offers or sells a fine print in violation of the Act shall be liable to the purchaser for the consideration paid for the print, plus interest at the legal rate, upon tender of delivery of the print. Furthermore, if the offer or sale was done "wilfully," recovery may be *trebled*.

There is an exception in the statute for moderately-priced prints; the Act does not apply to any print when offered for sale at wholesale or retail unframed for $25 or less or framed for $40 or less.

Although at present the statute has been enacted in California, it is not unlikely that other states will subsequently enact similar acts. Furthermore, inasmuch as any printmaker is likely to offer prints in various states he must be prepared to furnish the relevant "informational details" required by California.

ARTIST-ART DEALER RELATIONSHIPS

In 1969 New York passed a statute dealing with artist-art dealer relationships, which supplemented a prior abbreviated statute that was passed in 1966. The present statute provides that:

Any custom, practice or usage of the trade to the contrary notwithstanding, a) whenever an artist delivers or causes to be delivered a work of fine art of his own creation to an art dealer for the purpose of exhibition and/or sale on a commission, fee or other basis of compensation, the delivery to and acceptance thereof by the art dealer is deemed to be 'on consignment,' and

    i)   such art dealer shall thereafter, with respect to the said work of fine art, be deemed to be the agent of such artist, and

    ii)   such work of fine art is trust property in the hands of the consignee for the benefit of the consignor, and

    iii)   any proceeds from the sale of such work of fine art are trust funds in the hands of the consignee for the benefit of the consignor. . . .[2]

Furthermore, if the dealer (consignee) subsequently purchases the work on consignment, directly or indirectly for his own account, the work remains trust property until the full price is paid to the artist (consignor). If the work is then resold to a third party before the artist has been paid in full, the proceeds of the resale are trust funds in the hands of the dealer to be applied to any balance still due the artist.

Any artist may lawfully waive only that part of the statute which provides that "any proceeds from the sale of such work of fine art are trust funds in the hands of the consignee for the benefit of the consignor" *provided*:

    a)   that such waiver is clear, conspicuous, in writing and subscribed by the consignor;

    b)   that no waiver shall be valid with respect to the first $2,500 of gross proceeds of sales received in any twelve-month period commencing with the date of execution of such waiver; and

    c)   that no waiver shall be valid with respect to the proceeds of a work of fine art initially received 'on consignment' but subsequently purchased by the consignee directly or indirectly for his own account.

This statute and its predecessor, which were recommended by the New York State Attorney General, had as their principal purpose "to clarify the *inherently* fiduciary character of the 'consignment arrangement' in the artist-art dealer relationship (not to be confused with 'sales on consignment' where the resulting relationship resembles that of debtor and creditor rather than that of principal and agent)." As further stated by the Attorney General: "The abuses . . . necessitated legislation which would remove any residue of doubt as to the fiduciary nature of the consignment arrangement in the artist-art dealer relationship and lay the legal foundation for the application of criminal sanctions against embezzlement (larceny) of the principal's property. . . ."[3] (See Chapter 2 on the artist and his gallery.)

FALSIFICATION OF CERTIFICATES OF AUTHENTICITY

In 1969, the New York State Legislature passed a statute which provides that: "A person who, with intent to defraud, deceive or injure another, makes, utters or issues a false certificate of authenticity of a work of fine art" is guilty of a crime.[4] A "certificate of authenticity" is a written or printed statement of fact or opinion that confirms, approves or attests to the authenticity of the authorship of a work of fine art, which statement is subscribed by the authenticator and can be used to the advantage or disadvantage of some person.

While the purpose of this statute is not principally to protect the artist— but rather the buyer and collector of art—there may be situations where the artist or his family may be required to supply a certificate of authenticity. The statute does not discriminate among various persons who may deliver a false certificate, and would include the artist. It should be noted that the Act specifically refers to a false "opinion" as well as a statement of fact. Thus, if the authenticator issues a false opinion to support an income tax deduction for donation of a work of art to a museum, a violation of the statute would occur. Except for this statute, it appears that the falsification of written statements of opinion are not punishable under any existing category of crime.

ATTORNEY GENERAL'S POWER TO COMBAT FRAUD AND SEEK RESTITUTION

In 1970, the New York State Legislature, in two instances, enlarged[5] the Attorney General's power to apply to the courts for an order directing restitution to the aggrieved, as well as enjoining fraudulent or illegal business activity.

REPRESENTATIONS AND WARRANTIES OF WORKS OF ART

New York has passed another statute that affects principally the art collector, rather than the visual artist, but the statute has a relationship to anyone working as a visual artist. The key provision of the statute provides that:

Any provision in any other law to the contrary notwithstanding:
1. Whenever an art merchant, in selling or exchanging a work of fine art, furnishes to a buyer of such work who is not an art merchant, a written instrument which, in describing the work, identifies it with any author or authorship, such description (i) shall be presumed to be part of the basis of the bargain and (ii) shall create an express warranty of the authenticity of such authorship as of the date of such sale or exchange. Such warranty shall not be negated or limited because the seller in the written instrument did not use formal words such as 'warrant' or 'guarantee' or because he did not have a specific intention or authorization to make a warranty or

because any statement relevant to authorship is, or purports to be, or is capable of being merely the seller's opinion.

The term "art merchant" is defined as:

a person who deals in works of fine art or by his occupation holds himself out as having knowledge or skill peculiar to works of fine art or to whom such knowledge or skill may be attributed by his employment of an agent or broker or other intermediary who by his occupation holds himself out as having such knowledge or skill. The term 'art merchant' includes an auctioneer who sells works of fine art at public auction as well as such auctioneer's consignor or principal.[6]

The statute makes it clear that various written statements made in connection with the sale indicate, in accordance with customs in the trade, diverse degrees of authenticity. Thus, the Act takes into account the various discriminations in claims that may be made by a seller with respect to a work of art, such as "by a named (artist)," "attributed to a named (artist)," or "school of a named (artist)," each of which is given a meaning under the bill compatible with its accepted usage.

Disclaimers of warranty are prevented if: a) the work is proved to be a "counterfeit"—i.e., made in such a manner as to appear to have an authorship which it does not have, even though it may not have been made with an intent to deceive—and this was not clearly indicated in the description of the work[7] and b) the work is unqualifiedly stated to be the work of a named artist and it is found that, as of the date of sale or exchange, such statement was false, mistaken, or erroneous. Disclaimers would, however, be permitted with respect to other purported representations if they clearly and specifically apprise the buyer that the seller is assuming no risk or responsibility for the authenticity of the authorship of the work.

Stripped of its technical wording, the bill is aimed at preventing sophisticated sellers of art—so-called "art merchants"—from selling works purportedly by well-known names to unsophisticated buyers of art. As stated in the memorandum of the Attorny General recommending the law:

Under this bill the identification of a work of fine art with any authorship creates a presumption that such description of the work *is* part of the basis of the bargain. No formal words are required to prove that, to a buyer, authenticity of authorship is 'of the essence of the contract.' This bill recognizes what is axiomatic in the art market—buyers pay high prices for 'names.'[8]

REPRODUCTION RIGHTS

In 1966, New York enacted a statute[9] which provides that unless otherwise agreed a creator of a work of fine art reserves the right of reproduction.

The purpose of the statute was to reverse a 1942 ruling of The New York Court of Appeals in the case of *Pushman v. New York Graphic Society, Inc.,*[10] in which it was held that an artist who gave an absolute and unconditional bill of sale of an uncopyrighted painting retains no such common law copyright as to enable him to prevent commercial reproduction or exploitation by the purchaser.

Various lawyers in the copyright field have suggested that the statute may conflict with the federal copyright statute and United States Constitution in its implication that the artist retains the reproduction rights to the work (without an express grant) even though the artist by his sale may have "published" the work.[11] It seems clear, however, from a reading of the *Pushman* case that that case, which dealt only with a painting "not copyrighted under the copyright laws of the United States," was concerned only with "the so-called common law copyright, not statutory copyright." Further, the New York State Attorney General, who had proposed the statute, stated in his legislative memorandum to the Governor that the proposal was "designed merely to overcome the effect of the *Pushman* case" and referred expressly to an "uncopyrighted painting" and "common law copyright."[12] It has been pointed out that in implementing the constitutional mandate, Congress has not seen fit to pre-empt the entire area of copyright, limiting federal jurisdiction in the main to published works.[13] Moreover, Section 2 of the Copyright Act provides: "Nothing in this title shall be construed to annul or limit the right of the author or proprietor of an unpublished work, at common law or in equity, to prevent the copying, publication or use of such unpublished work without his consent, and to obtain damages therefore."[14] It would, therefore, appear that in those situations where the sale or exhibition of the art work did not constitute a "publication" of the work within the meaning of the federal copyright statute—as, for example, by limiting its use, preventing any photographing of the work, or the like—the statute has limited vitality,[15] although unquestionably its protective shield for the artist is inferior[16] to that provided by compliance with the federal copyright notice requirements.*

EXEMPTION OF WORKS OF ART FROM SEIZURE

As a general rule, a plaintiff-creditor in a lawsuit may "seize" any property of a non-resident defendant that he may find in the jursidction. In 1968, a statute was enacted in New York that exempts from seizure:

> any work of fine art while the same is enroute to or from, or while on exhibition or deposited by a non-resident exhibitor at any exhibition held under the auspices or supervision of any museum,

---

*See Chapter 1.

college, university or other non-profit art gallery, institution or organization ... for any cultural, educational, charitable or other purpose not conducted for profit to the exhibitor. . . .[17]

The purpose of the law was to extend a precedent that granted a similar exemption to purely commercial exhibits at international exhibitions held under the auspices of the United States.

The philosophy underlying the statute was aptly described by the Attorney General who had sponsored the bill:

If New York is to retain its recently acquired leadership in this century as a cultural center, it is important to treat art exhibitions of national, as well as international significance, with at least the same degree of consideration as a World's Fair. It is precisely such art exhibitions which have changed New York from a provincial to an international art center. Such exhibitions depend upon borrowing works of fine art from public and private collections as well as artists from all over this nation and from all parts of the world. Under existing law such exhibits may be seized, attached or sequestered by local creditors. The non-residence of the exhibitor, whose property may be impounded by the sheriff even while such exhibition is in progress, makes him prey to harrassment which he could easily avoid by refusing to lend his property in the first instance for exhibitions in this State. This bill would remove such fear of harrassment on the part of lenders of works of fine art which might tend to discourage foreign exhibits from crossing state or national boundaries into the State of New York.

It is to be noted that this bill is aimed at protecting foreign exhibits only when shipped here in connection with a purely cultural exhibition and does not affect the rights of creditors of non-residents whose works are sent here for commercial exhibitions at art galleries where the works are for sale.[18]

APPENDIX: ORGANIZATIONS PROVIDING ASSISTANCE TO THE ARTIST

Associated Councils of the Arts
1564 Broadway
New York, New York 10036
212 586-3731

Associated Councils of the Arts is a nonprofit, membership service corporation. As a public foundation under the Tax Reform Act of 1969 it conducts programs of research, communications, and action to help secure for the arts their proper position among the priorities of the peoples of North America. ACA works closely with its member councils, with other arts organizations, and with individuals and functions as spokesman on issues that affect all the arts.

ACA conducts conferences on issues of national importance and seminars on matters of special interest. It serves as a secretariat for the Council of National Arts Organizations Executives and also for Volunteer Lawyers for the Arts. ACA publishes *ACA Reports*, a monthly newsletter on arts activities; *ACA Word from Washington*, a monthly rundown on legislation that touches the arts; occasional *ACA Specials*, books on various aspects of the arts. Two *ACA Specials* of interest are *Washington and the Arts: A Guide and Directory to Federal Programs and Dollars for the Arts* and a *Directory of National Arts Organizations* (revised editions of both due to be published in 1974).

ACA is supported through earned income, membership dues, and contributions from individuals, corporations, and foundations.

National Endowment for the Arts
1425 K Street, N.W.
Washington, D.C. 20506
202 382-6208

The National Foundation on the Arts and the Humanities was originally established as an independent agency of the Executive Branch of the federal government by the National Foundation on the Arts and the Humanities Act of 1965. The National Foundation is composed of the National Endowment for the Arts and the National Endowment for the Humanities. The two Endowments, advised by their respective Councils, formulate their own programs, but share an administrative staff.

The National Endowment for the Arts carries out programs of grants-in-aid given to arts agencies of the states and territories, to nonprofit, tax-exempt organizations and to individuals of exceptional talent.

Grants by the Endowment to the states and territories are administered by the individual arts agencies. The Endowment's own programs are developed by the chairman and the staff, with the advice of the National Council on the Arts, which is headed by the chairman of the Endowment. As a general rule, applications for grants which fall within the established programs of the Endowment are referred to panels of experts chosen from all regions of the United States. The recommendations of the panels are brought before the National Council for review and to the chairman for final determination.

Volunteer Lawyers for the Arts
36 West 44th Street
New York, New York 10036
212 247-4390

Located in New York, Volunteer Lawyers for the Arts conducts programs of service to New York's artistic community. It also has programs of nation-wide interest and cooperates on joint projects with volunteer attorney groups in other areas.

VLA coordinates the volunteer activities of lawyers on behalf of the arts in an effort to avail New York's indigent artists and arts groups of the kind of legal advice they so often need in order to function. To participate in this program, the artist or arts group must have a legal problem closely related to his or its artistic pursuits and must be financially unable to engage an attorney. No fee is ever collected by a volunteer for the services performed in this program. However, once the artist or arts group becomes financially able to hire a lawyer, VLA-sponsored assistance is terminated.

VLA also coordinates volunteer legal representation in matters affecting artists as a class. In such cases volunteers may draft model contracts and model legislation or seek assistance and clarification from government agencies which administer laws affecting a class of artists. In its research and publication efforts VLA has cooperated with the Art Committee of The Association of the Bar of the City of New York and Associated Councils of the Arts in producing this monograph. Monographs are also planned on the insurance, tax, and accounting considerations for individual artists and art groups, and a handbook dealing with artists' housing in the SoHo district in New York City. Research is done by committees of lawyers drawn from the organization's roster of volunteers. VLA has initiated a program on on-going legislative monitoring of bills affecting the arts proposed for legislation in various bellwether states and is also engaged in sponsoring seminars on topics of current interest in arts related law.

State Arts Councils

The first state arts council was established in 1902. Six other councils had been formed by 1960, when the New York State Council of the Arts was created and received the first major funding. Today, legislatively created councils exist in every state and territory with budgets totalling more than $27 million.

The councils are funded by appropriations from state legislatures, contributions from the National Endowment for the Arts, and matching grants. Their programs are designed to stimulate creative and interpretive works on the one hand, and an audience for them on the other.

Alabama State Council on the Arts and Humanities
322 Alabama Street, Montgomery 36104

Alaska State Council on the Arts
338 Denali Street, Anchorage 99501

Arizona Commission on the Arts and Humanities
6330 North Seventh Street, Phoenix 85014

Arkansas State Council on the Arts and Humanities
Union Station
Little Rock 72201

California Arts Commission
808 "O" Street, Sacramento 95814

The Colorado Council on the Arts and Humanities
Room 205, 1550 Lincoln Street, Denver 80203

Connecticut Commission on the Arts
340 Capitol Avenue, Hartford 06106

Delaware State Arts Council
601 Delaware Avenue, Wilmington 19801

District of Columbia Commission on the Arts
Room 543, Munsey Building, 1329 E Street, N.W. 20004

Fine Arts Council of Florida
Department of State, the Capitol Building, Tallahassee 32304

Georgia Council for the Arts
706 Peachtree Center South Building
225 Peachtree Street, N.E., Atlanta 30303

Hawaii—The State Foundation on Culture and the Arts
Room 310, 250 South King Street, Honolulu 96813

Idaho State Commission on the Arts and Humanities
Suite 322, Annex #3, Old St. Al's Hospital, Boise 83701

Illinois Arts Council
Room 1610, 111 North Wabash Avenue, Chicago 60602

Indiana Arts Commission
Suite 707, Thomas Building
15 East Washington Street, Indianapolis 46204

Iowa State Arts Council
State Capitol Building, Des Moines 50319

Kansas Arts Commission
120 North Oliver Street, Wichita 67208

Kentucky Arts Commission
Main & High Streets, Frankfort 40601

Louisiana Council for Music and Performing Arts
611 Gravier Street, New Orleans 70130

Maine State Commission on the Arts and Humanities
State House, Augusta 04330

Maryland Arts Council
15 West Mulberry Street, Baltimore 21201

Massachusetts Council on the Arts and Humanities
14 Beacon Street, Boston 02108

Michigan Council for the Arts
10125 East Jefferson Avenue, Detroit 48214

Minnesota State Arts Council
100 East 22nd Street, Minneapolis 55404

Mississippi Arts Commission
P.O. Box 1341, Jackson 39205

Missouri State Council on the Arts
Suite 410, 111 South Bemistor, St. Louis 63105

Montana Arts Council
Room 310, Fine Arts Building,
University of Montana, Missoula 59801

Nebraska Arts Council
P.O. Box 1536, Omaha 68101

Nevada State Council on the Arts
P.O. Box 208, Reno 89504

New Hampshire Commission on the Arts
Phoenix Hall, North Main Street, Concord 03301

New Jersey State Council on the Arts
27 West State Street, Trenton 08608

New Mexico Arts Commission
Lew Wallace Building, State Capitol, Santa Fe 87501

New York State Council on the Arts
250 West 57th Street, New York 10019

North Carolina Arts Council
Room 245, 101 North Person Street, Raleigh 27601

North Dakota Council on the Arts and Humanities
North Dakota State University, Fargo 58102

Ohio Arts Council
Room 2840, 50 West Broad Street, Columbus 43215

Oklahoma Arts and Humanities Council
1140 N.W. 63rd Street, Oklahoma City 73116

Oregon Arts Commission
328 Oregon Building, 494 State Street, Salem 97310

Commonwealth of Pennsylvania Council on the Arts
503 North Front Street, Harrisburg 17101

Rhode Island State Council on the Arts
4365 Post Road, East Greenwich 02818

South Carolina Arts Commission
1205 Pendleton Street, Columbia 29201

South Dakota State Fine Arts Council
108 West 11th Street, Sioux Falls 57102

Tennessee Arts Commission
Room 222, Capitol Hill Building, Nashville 37219

Texas Commission on the Arts and Humanities
403 East Sixth Street, Austin 78701

Utah State Institute of Fine Arts
609 East South Temple Street, Salt Lake City 84102

Vermont Council on the Arts
136 State Street, Montpelier 05602

Virginia Commission on the Arts and Humanities
1214 State Office Building, Richmond 23219

Washington State Arts Commission
1151 Black Lake Boulevard, Olympia 98504

West Virginia Arts and Humanities Council
State Office Building No. 6, Room B-531
1900 Washington Street East, Charleston 25305

Wisconsin Arts Council
P.O. Box 3356, Madison 53704

Wyoming Council on the Arts
200 West 25th Street, Cheyenne 82002

NOTES

CHAPTER 1

1. *Letter Edged in Black Press v. Public Building Commission*, 320 F. Supp. 1303 (N.D. Ill. 1970).

2. See generally M. Nimmer, *Nimmer on Copyright* (1972 ed.) [hereinafter cited as *Nimmer*], §§ 100, 101, 141.2, 143, pp. 374-383.4, 613-614, 619-643, and cases cited therein.

3. See ibid., § 49, pp. 193-196, and cases cited therein.

4. 17 U.S.C. §§ 1, 24.

5. A good representative group is *Nimmer*; A. Latman, *Howell's Copyright Law* (Rev. ed. 1962); B. Ringer and P. Gitlin, *Copyrights* (Rev. ed. 1965). An excellent brief discussion is contained in the pamphlet, "Copyright in Works of Art," prepared by Joshua Binion Cahn for Artists Equity Association (2d ed. 1956).

6. U.S. Const. Art. 1, § 8, clause 8 given the power to "Congress to promote the Progress of . . . Useful Arts, by securing for limited Times to Authors . . . the exclusive Right to their respective Writings. . . ." An interesting question theoretically presented by this language is whether the *"Useful Arts"* includes the visual arts (paintings, graphics, and sculpture) and whether artists and their works are encompassed under the Constitutional terms "Authors" and "Writings." It is clearly settled by court decisions and statutes, however, that fine art and artists and included within the Constitutional protection. See, for example, *Nimmer*, §§ 6.2, 8.2, pp. 11, 16-18; *Monogram Models, Inc. v. Industro Motive Corp.*, 448 F.2d 284, 287-288 (6th Cir. 1971); *Columbia Broadcasting System, Inc. v. DeCosta*, 377 F.2d 315, 320 (1st Cir.), cert. denied, 389 U.S. 1007 (1967), stating that a constitutional "Writing" includes "any concrete, describable manifestation of intellectual creation. . . ."

7. 17 U.S.C. § 19.

8. 17 U.S.C. § 20.

9. 17 U.S.C. § 16.

10. *Allegrini v. DeAngelis*, 59 F. Supp. 248 (E.D. Pa. 1944), *aff'd*, 149 F.2d 815 (3d Cir. 1945); *Alva Studios Inc. v. Winninger*, 177 F. Supp. 265 (S.D. N.Y. 1959).

11. *Nimmer*, §§ 143.11, 166, pp. 620-626.2, 714-716, and cases cited therein.

12. *Duff v. The Kansas City Star Co.*, 299 F.2d 320 (8th Cir. 1962); *Becker v. Loew's, Inc.*, 133 F.2d 889 (7th Cir.), *cert. denied*, 319 U.S. 772 (1943).

13. *Nimmer*, § 37, pp. 147-162.

14. 17 U.S.C. § 9.

15. 17 U.S.C. § 16.

16. *Nimmer*, § 145, pp. 643-654.

17. *Rosemont Enterprises, Inc. v. Random House, Inc.*, 366 F.2d 303, 306-310 (2d Cir. 1966), *cert. denied*, 385 U.S. 1009 (1967); *Eisenschimil v. Fawcett Publications, Inc.*, 246 F.2d 598 (7th Cir.), *cert. denied*, 355 U.S. 907 (1957); *Holdredge v. Knight Publishing Corp.*, 214 F. Supp. 921 (S.D. Cal. 1963).

18. The design patent statutes are found in 35 U.S.C. §§ 171-173. An exact delineation of the difference in subject matter coverage between design patents and copyrights is not possible. In some cases a work of art may be eligible for both types of coverage. A discussion of the overlapping coverage and whether or not an election must be made is found in *Nimmer*, § 38, pp. 162-164.

19. The Universal Copyright Convention is set forth in full in *Nimmer*, Ap. K, pp. 989-100.1 and 6 U.S.T. 2731. Art. II of the Convention sets forth the rights acquired through use of the prescribed copyright notice.

20. The Berne Convention is set forth in full in *Nimmer*, Ap. O, pp. 1017-1032. Art. 4 of the Convention sets forth the rights acquired by following the prescribed procedure. The Berne Convention was revised in Stockholm in 1967 and in Paris on July 24, 1971. The revised text (generally referred to as the Paris text) has not yet entered into force. See *Nimmer*, § 65.64, p. 266 n. 192. The Paris text is set forth in full in *Nimmer*, Ap. P, pp, 1033-1071. Article 5 of the Paris text states the rights which may be acquired.

21. The Buenos Aires Convention is set forth in full in *Nimmer*, Ap. M, pp. 1003-1006 and 38 Statutes at Large 1785. Art. 3 of the Convention sets forth the rights acquired by use of the prescribed notice.

22. N.Y. Gen. Bus. L. Art. 12-E.

23. *Pushman v. New York Graphic Society, Inc.*, 287 N.Y. 302, 39 N.E.2d 249 (1942), discussed in detail in Chapter 8, p. 63.

24. 17 U.S.C. § 27.

25. *Gottsberger v. Aldine Book Publishing Co.*, 33 F. 381 (C.C.D. Mass. 1887); *Nimmer*, § 49, p. 195. *Cf. Pushman v. New York Graphic Society, Inc.*, *(supra*, Ch. 1, n. 23).

26. See *Scherr v. Universal Match Corp.*, 297 Supp. 107, 112 (S.D. N.Y. 1967), *aff'd*, 417 F.2d 497 (2d Cir. 1969), *cert. denied*, 397 U.S. 936 (1970); *Nimmer*, § 54, pp. 212-213.

27. *American Tobacco Co. v. Werckmeister*, 207 U.S. 284 (1907); *Werckmeister v. American Lithographic Co.*, *134 F. 321* (2d Cir. 1904); *Nimmer*, § 58, p. 224. *Cf.* Ch. 1, n. 28, and Ch. 7, n. 54, *infra.*

28. *See Price, Government Policy and Economic Security for Artists: The Case of the Droit de Suite*, 77 Yale L. J. 1333, at 1345 n. 32 (1968): "What constitutes publication is uncertain because of the paucity of litigation; the effect of displaying a work in a gallery or museum is still not settled." *Cf.* Ch. 8, n. 11, *infra.*

29. 17 U.S.C. § 19.

30. The Copyright Act only requires that the year of first publication appear in the copyright notice where the subject matter is printed literary, musical, or dramatic works and sound recordings. 17 U.S.C. § 19. With regard to other copyrightable works, there is no requirement that the year of first publication be included. *Nimmer*, § 85.1, p. 307. The Universal Copyright Convention (Art. III (1)), however, requires a statement of the year in connection with all works. Thus, the distinction between the different types of works drawn in the Copyright Act is relatively unimportant where international protection is desired, and the year of first publication should consequently be included in the copyright notice without regard to the subject matter.

31. See 17 U.S.C. § 19; *Nimmer*, § 82, pp. 302-304.

32. The "short form" may also be used on maps, models or designs for works of art, drawings or plastic works of scientific or technical character. *Compare* 17 U.S.C. § 19 *with* 17 U.S.C. § 5 (f)-(k).

33. 17 U.S.C. § 19.

34. See Ch. 1, n. 30 *supra.*

35. See generally *Nimmer*, § 65.34, pp. 259-260 and the Buenos Aires Convention (*supra* Ch. 1, n. 21), Art. 3.

36. *Coventry Ware, Inc. v. Reliance Picture Frame Co.*, 288 F.2d 193 (2d Cir. 1961); Ch. 4, Sec. 4.3.6. Compendium of Copyright Office Practices, U.S. Copyright Office, July 1, 1970.

37. *Nimmer*, § 87.7, p, 323.

38. *Id.* See also *Nimmer*, § 87.5, pp. 322-323.

39. *Nimmer*, § 87.8, pp. 324-325.

40. *Nimmer*, § 119.32, pp. 518-521. *Goodis v. United Artists Television, Inc.*, 425 F.2d 397 (2d Cir. 1970).

41. Absent registration, a statutory copyright cannot be enforced. 17 U.S.C. § 13. Regarding demand by the copyright office, see 17 U.S.C. § 14. Renewals are governed by 17 U.S.C. §§ 24, 25.

42. See 17 U.S.C. § 215. The fee for registering a claim to a copyright for any work is $6. *Id.*

43. 17 U.S.C. § 13. The copies must conform in all respects to those published, including placement of the copyright notice. *Nimmer,* § 92.2, pp. 347-348.

44. *Id.* For procedure see 37 C.F.R. § 202.16 (1959), and item 4 of Form G, a copy of which appears at the end of this chapter.

45. 17 U.S.C. § 15.

46. 17 U.S.C. § 28.

47. *Nimmer,* § 120.1, p. 552.1, and cases cited therein. An assignment of a common law copyright may also be implied from conduct. *Id.*

48. 17 U.S.C. § 30. Absent such filing, the assignment is "void as against any subsequent purchaser or mortgagee for valuable consideration, without notice, whose assignment has been duly recorded." *Id.*

49. *Id.*

50. 17 U.S.C. § 28.

CHAPTER 2

1. In addition to traditional galleries, there are agents who avoid the overhead costs of maintaining gallery spaces open to the public and concentrate their efforts on a selected list of potential purchasers. See *Price (supra* Ch. 1, n, 30), at 1342. The material treated in this chapter will be largely applicable to such an agent.

2. N.Y. Gen. Bus. L. Art. 12-C. See Chapter 8, pp. 58-59.

3. For an extensive article on *droit de suite*, see *Price (supra* Ch. 1, n. 30).

4. The form was developed by Robert Projansky (a lawyer) and Seth Siegelaub (publisher of art books and formerly a dealer); copies of the form may be obtained from Mr. Siegelaub at P.O. Box 350, New York, New York 10013.

5. See article by George J. Benston in Wall Street Journal, April 21, 1971, p. 22. Mr. Benston, a professor of economics at the University of Rochester School of Management, describes himself as "a lover of art and a very minor collector." *Cf. Price (supra* Ch. 1, n. 30) at 1364-1366.

CHAPTER 3

1. *Webster's Seventh New Collegiate Dictionary*, G. & C. Merriam Co. (1969).

2. Elisabeth Stevens, Wall Street Journal, January 5, 1971, p. 14.

3. A. Lindey, *Entertainment, Publishing and the Arts* (1963, Cum. Supp. 1972), pp. 783-784 [hereinafter cited as *Lindey*].

4. *Id.*, p. 785.

5. *Id.*, pp. 789-790.

6. E.g., Random House, Inc., Standard form of Art Contract (1969).

7. E.g., Thomas Y. Crowell Company, Standard form of Art Contract (1968).

8. E.g., Doubleday and Company, Inc., Form of Memorandum of Agreement (1969).

9. See Ch. 3, n. 7 *supra.*

10. 17 U.S.C. § 16.

11. See 28 Op. Att'y Gen. 150 (1910); 28 Op. Att'y Gen. 557 (1911); *Ringer and Gitlin (supra* Ch. 1, n. 5), pp. 44-45.

12. See Ch. 3, ns. 6, 8, and 9 *supra.*

13. *Lindey*, pp. 784, 790.

14. E.g., William R. Scott, Inc., Standard form of Artist's Contract (1970).

15. *Lindey*, p. 795.

16. See Ch. 3, n. 7 *supra.*

17. Ibid.

18. *Lindey*, pp. 786, 791.

19. Ibid.

20. See note Ch. 3, n. 7 *supra.*

CHAPTER 4

1. *Pushman v. New York Graphic Society, Inc.*, 287 N.Y. 302, 39 N.E.2d 249 (1942).

2. *Grant v. Kellogg Co.*, 58 F. Supp. 48 (D.C. N.Y. 1944), *aff'd*, 154 F.2d 59 (2d Cir. 1946).

3. *Lindey*, pp. 467-468.

4. N. Y. Gen. Bus. L. Art. 12-E, § 224.

5. N. Y. Unif. Comm. Code § 2-509.

6. Ibid., and § 2-503.

7. *Deitch v. Shamash*, 56 Misc. 2d 875, 290 N.Y.S.2d 137 (Civ. Ct. 1968).

8. N.Y. Unif. Comm. Code § 2-509.

9. See N. Y. Gen. Bus. L. Arts. 12-D and 12-F, discussed in Chapter 8, p. 61.

10. S. Hodes, *The Law of Art and Antiques* (1966), pp. 1-2 [hereinafter cited as *Hodes*].

11. *Id.*, p. 5

12. *Id.*, p. 3.

13. Ibid.

14. *Id.*, p. 4.

CHAPTER 5

1. Nochlin, *Museum and Radicals: A History of Emergencies*, Art in America (July-August 1971), p. 26.

2. See Leavitt. *The Beleaguered Director*, Art in America (July-August 1971), pp, 66-67; Glueck, *Power and Esthetics: The Trustee*, Art in America (July-August 1971), p. 78.

3. See Robertson, *The Museum and the Democratic Fallacy*, Art in America (July-August 1971), p. 58; Kozloff, *Under the Corporate Wing*, Art in America (July-August 1971), p. 92.

4. See Fry, *The Dilemmas of the Curator*, Art in America (July-August 1971), pp. 72, 77.

5. Joint Artists-Museums Committee, *The Museum and the Artist* 19-20 (1958).

6. N.Y. Gen. Bus. L. Art. 12-E, §§ 223, 224. See Chapter 8, pp. 62-63, for an extended discussion of this statute.

7. *Lindey*, p. 19.

8. B. Hollander, *The International Law of Art* (1959), p. 234.

9. Am. Jur. 2d Bailments, §§ 120, 206.

10. New York Times, January 4, 1969, p. 24, col. 3.

11. Rago, *The Moral Rights of the Author; A Comparative Study*, 71 Dick. L. Rev. 93 (1966).

12. Sarraute, *Current Theory of the Moral Right of Authors and Artists under French Law*, 16 Am. J. Comp. L. 465 (1969).

13. Devlin, *Moral Right in the United States*, 35 Conn. B. J. 509-510 (1961).

14. Roeder, *The Doctrine of Moral Right: A Study in the Law of Artists, Authors and Creators*, 53 Harv. L. Rev. 554 (1940).

15. Decision of Cour d'Appel de Paris, reported in Recueil Periodique et Critique Dalloz, 1931. II. 88. (March 6, 1931).

16. Decision of Cour decassation, reported in Gazette du Palais, Jurisprudence, 1965. II. 126. (July 6, 1965).

17. Treece, *American Law Analogues of the Author's "Moral Right,"* 16 Am. J. Comp. L. 487, 499 (1968).

18. N. Y. Educ. L. § 264.

19. *Hodes*, p. 10.

20. Ibid.

CHAPTER 6

1. Artists working in New York City are subject to the 4 percent New York City tax imposed on their unincorporated business taxable income allocable to the City for their

taxable years beginning on or after January 1, 1971. An exemption of $5,000 and a deduction (not in excess of either $5,000 or 20 percent of taxable income before deductions or exemptions) for reasonable compensation of the proprietor's personal services are allowed in computing taxable income as well as a tax credit for the benefit of small taxpayers. In sum, artists who have taxable income, before exemptions and credits, of $7,500 or less will not be responsible for any tax. N.Y.C. Adm. Code, Tit. S, c. 46, as amended by L. L. 36, Laws 1971. Artists and other professionals, however, still remain exempt from the state unincorporated business tax. It appears, however, that a commercial artist, as contrasted with a fine artist, is not considered engaged in a "profession" and accordingly is subject to the state tax. See *Wilson v. Bates*, 282 App. Div. 1099, 126 N.Y.S. 2d 550 (3d. Dept. 1953), appeal denied, 306 N.Y. 985, 118 N.E. 2d 607 (1954); *White v. Murphy*, 11 App. Div. 2d 854, 203 N.Y.S. 2d 44 (3d. Dept. 1960), att'd 9 N.Y. 2d 995, 218 N.Y.S. 2d 67 (1961).

2. Internal Revenue Code of 1954, as amended ("Code") § 61.

3. Code § 1.

4. Code §§ 1001, 1002, 1011, 62, 63, and Treasury Regulations ("Regs.") § 1.471-3.

5. Code §§ 1221, 1222.

6. Code § 1202.

7. Code § 1221 (1), (3).

8. Code § 1001 (b).

9. Code §§ 1001, 1002, 1012.

10. Code § 1221 (3). This is to be contrasted with an inventor assigning his patent, which generally would permit capital gains treatment. See Code § 1235. This difference in treatment has been criticized by art organizations, such as Artists Equity Association of New York, Inc. A bill has recently been introduced in Congress to give capital gains treatment to the transfer of a copyright or a literary, musical, or *artistic* composition. See H.R. 843, 92d Cong., 1st Sess. (1971).

11. Code § 451, Regs. § 1.451-1. In some cases no income will be realized until the cost of producing the work has been recouped, *Burnet v. Logan*, 283 U. S. 404 (1931), and then income will be realized only as received.

12. Code §§ 1301, 1302, 1303.

13. The successful artist, who may have been casually advised to incorporate himself, must be aware of the prohibitive 70 percent tax on undistributed personal holding company income. Code § 541. A corporation is a personal holding company if it meets two tests: 1) more than 50 percent in value of its outstanding stock is owned directly or indirectly by five or fewer individuals and 2) 60 percent or more of its "adjusted ordinary gross income" for the year is personal holding company income. In determining stock ownership, an individual is considered to own stock owned by a spouse, brother, sister, ancestor, lineal descendant, or partner. Code § 544 (a) (2).

14. Code § 1348.

15. Code §§ 1348 (b), 401 (c) (2) (C). *But see* Rev. Rul. 71-183, I.R.B. 1971-15, 15.

16. Code § 401.

17. Code § 404 (e).

18. Code § 501.

19. Code § 402.

20. Code § 72 (n).

21. Code § 401 (c) (2). See Ch. 6, n. 15 *supra.*

22. Code §§ 62, 165, 1011, 1012, Regs. § 1.471-3.

23. Code § 1033.

24. Code § 162; *Van Pickeril & Sons, Inc. v. United States*, 70-1 U.S.T.C. ¶ 9391 (S.D. Ill. 1970).

25. Code § 170.

26. Code § 170 (e); H.R. Rep. No. 91-413 (Part I), 91st Cong., 1st Sess. 53 (1969). This provision has been criticized severely by artists. See, for example, the October 1970

issue of the Newsletter published by Artists Equity Association of New York, Inc., which exclaims: "The only answer the artist can give to this demeaning law is to *stop contributing works of art to all institutions!*" (emphasis in original).

27. Code § 170 (e), Regs. § 1.170-1 (c). However, under § 170 (e), if an art object or other tangible property is donated, 50 percent of its appreciation in value will not be usable by the donor as a tax deduction (62.5 percent if the donor is a corporation) unless the charity "uses" it, or is reasonably expected to "use" it, in connection with its tax-exempt function. For example, if a museum is given a painting costing $1,000 and worth $5,000, the full $5,000 deduction should be available to the donor if the museum is expected to display it; but only a $3,000 deduction may be available ($5,000 less 50 percent of the $4,000 appreciation) if the museum plans to sell it right away. Similarly, a gift of a painting to a school that in fact is used for educational purposes (display and study) will permit the full deduction.

28. Code §§ 1221 (3) (C), 1014, 170 (e), 1223 (2).

29. Code § 170.

30. Rev. Rul. 55-531, 1955-2 CUM. BULL. 520, *but see* Rev. Rul. 63-66, 1963-1 CUM. BULL. 13.

31. Code § 2522.

32. Code §§ 2503 (b), 2513.

33. Code § 2521.

34. Code § 2513, *but see* Rev. Rul. 54-30, 1954-1 CUM. BULL. 207.

35. Code § 2501 (a).

36. Code § 1221 (3).

37. Code §§ 2001, 2051.

38. Code §§ 2033-2044.

39. Code § 2041.

40. Code §§ 2031, 2032.

41. Code § 2056.

42. Regs. §§ 1.170-1 (c), 20.2031-1 (b), 25.2512-1.

43. Since artwork is characteristically sold through dealers, it has been argued that the value of a work should be the price that the artist will receive from a dealer and not from the ultimate purchaser, reflecting the normal reduction for the dealer's commission (ranging from 20 percent to 60 percent) for effecting the sale. *Cf.* Comments of Ralph Colin, administrative vice president and counsel of the Art Dealers Association, in 2d Hearings on Art Fraud Investigation, Office of the New York Attorney General, at 45-46. ("What would a dealer, faced with the hazards of the market" pay for the work?) In *Estate of David Smith*, 57 T.C.–(1972), CCH Fed. Est. & Gift Tax Rep. ¶ 8521, however, the court specifically rejected this argument and ruled that commissions payable are not deductible for estate tax purposes. The court held that the measure of value is the amount that could be received and not the amount that is retained from a hypothetical sale. In the same case, the court also rejected the argument that the value of an artist's works left in bulk could be discounted to reflect the price when sold to a bulk purchaser for resale. In determining the fair market value, the court considered the following factors: (1) the extent to which the sales price for each item would be affected by the quantity of the artist's works offered for sale at about the same time; (2) the extent to which the artist's reputation has developed; (3) the acceptance of the style of the art works in commercial markets; (4) the type, sales price and size of the artist's works; and (5) the distance at which the works are located from their markets. To the extent that it is necessary for the executors or administrators of the estate to dispose of the work in order properly to administer the estate, the commission expenses are deductible pursuant to the provisions of Reg. § 20.2053-3. The expenses are deductible "if the sale is necessary in order to pay the decedent's debts, expenses of administration, or taxes, to preserve the estate, or to effect distribution." *Estate of David Smith, supra.*

44. *Estate of W. A. Brown*, 21 CCH Tax Ct. Mem. 1321 (1962).

45. Regs. § 20.2031-6 (b).

46. IRS News Release, February 1, 1968, 687 CCH ¶ 6573.

47. See Ch. 6, n. 41 *supra*, and N . Y. EPTL § 11-1.1.

48. Code § 1401.

49. 42 U.S.C. § 402 (a), (g) (1) and (9).

50. 42 U.S.C. § § 402, 414.

51. 42 U.S.C. § 403 (f) (3). There is a special provision whereby royalties received after age 65 from a copyright or a patent obtained before age 65 are excluded from the computation of current income. S.S.A. § 203 (f) (5) (D) (ii). It has been urged that art created without benefit of copyright should have equal treatment. See booklet prepared by Emanuel Redfield for Artists Equity Association of New York, Inc., *Artists' Estates and Taxes*, p. 16.

52. S.S.A. § 203 (F) (1).

CHAPTER 7

1. The First Amendment applies directly to prohibit only federal restrictions of free speech. The Fourteenth Amendment, however, has been held by the Supreme Court to restrict state action to the same extent. See *Cantwell v. Connecticut*, 310 U.S. 296 (1940).

2. *Cox v. Louisiana*, 379 U.S. 536 (1965).

3. *Stromberg v. California*, 283 U.S. 359 (1931).

4. *Tinker v. Des Moines*, 393 U.S. 503 (1969).

5. *Memoirs v. Massachusetts*, 383 U.S. 413 (1966).

6. *Joseph Burstyn, Inc. v. Wilson*, 343 U.S. 495 (1952).

7. *Korn v. Elkins*, 317 F. Supp. 138 (D. Md. 1970); *Close v. Lederle*, 303 F. Supp. 1109 (D. Mass. 1969), *rev'd*, 424 F.2d 988 (1st Cir.), *cert. denied*, 400 U.S. 903 (1970).

8. *Chaplinsky v. New Hampshire*, 315 U.S. 568, 571-572 (1942) with *Cohen v. California*, 403 U.S. 15 (1971).

9. See *People v. Radich*, 26 N.Y.2d 114, 308 N.Y.S.2d 846, 257 N.E.2d 30 (1970), *aff'd by equally divided Court*, 401 U.S. 531 (1971). *Cf. Close v. Lederle* (*supra* Ch. 7, n. 7).

10. *United States v. O'Brien*, 391 U.S. 367 (1968).

11. Greater emphasis is being placed on the denial of First Amendment protection to the expression of ideas to a "captive audience." See *Cohen v. California* (supra Ch. 7, n. 8); *Close v. Lederle, supra* note 177; Brief of Appellee before Supreme Court, *Radich v. New York*, 401 U.S. 531 (1971).

12. In New York, even with adult supervision, a child may not be allowed to enter an exhibition with nude art works. N.Y. Pen. L. § 235.21.

13. *Watson v. Memphis*, 373 U.S. 526, 535 (1963).

14. *Winters v. New York*, 333 U.S. 507, 510 (1948).

15. *N. Y. Times Co. v. Sullivan*, 376 U.S. 254, 265-66 (1964); *Smith v. California*, 361 U.S. 147, 150 (1959).

16. See Monaghan, *First Amendment "Due Process,"* 83 Harv. L. Rev. 518-519 (1970).

17. *A Quantity of Books v. Kansas*, 378 U.S. 205 (1964); *Cambist Films, Inc. v. Duggan*, 420 F.2d 687 (3d Cir. 1969); *Bethview Amusement Corp. v. Cahn*, 416 F.2d 40 (2d Cir. 1969), *cert. denied*, 397 U.S. 920 (1970); *Tyrone, Inc. v. Wilkinson*, 410 F.2d 639 (4th Cir. 1969), *cert. denied*, 396 U.S. 985 (1969); *cf. Blount v. Rizzi*, 400 U.S. 410 (1971).

18. *Marcus v. Search Warrant*, 367 U.S. 717 (1961). See also cases cited in note 17 *supra*.

19. *Stanley v. Georgia*, 394 U.S. 557 (1969); *United States v. Various Articles of "Obscene" Merchandise*, 315 F. Supp. 191 (S.D. N.Y. 1970), *app. dism'd*, 400 U.S. 935 (1971).

20. *Bivens v. Six Unknown Named Agents of the Federal Bureau of Narcotics*, 403 U.S. 388 (1971); *Monroe v. Pape*, 365 U.S. 167 (1961). There is some question whether damages will be granted unless there has been actual violence by police officers. *Cf. Monroe v. Pape, supra, with Damico v. California*, 389 U.S. 416 (1967). In the event of continued harassment by police, an injunction might be obtainable. *See Bivens v. Six Unknown Named Agents of*

the Federal Bureau of Narcotics, 409 F.2d 718, 723 (2d Cir. 1969), *rev'd on other grounds*, 403 U.S. 388 (1971).

21. See, *e.g.*, N.Y. Gen. Bus. L. § 136; 18 Penn. Stat. § 4211; 18 U.S.C. § 700. See also Prosser, *Desecration of the American Flag*, 3 Ind. Legal Forum 160, 198-99, n. 208 (1969). The foregoing statutes seem to have been enacted in their present form for the purpose of outlawing political uses of the flag. Prior to 1968, there was no federal criminal statute relating to flag desecration. The first flag desecration statutes, enacted by states at the beginning of this century, were aimed at commercial and advertising uses of the flag. For a recent statute prescribing "rules for the display and use" of the American flag on public buildings, see N.Y. Exec. L. Art. 19, § 400 *et seq*.

22. A housewife on Long Island, New York, was prosecuted for flying an American flag upside-down to protest the war in Vietnam, while a local veterans group was not prosecuted for doing the same thing in protest against a conciliatory decision of the United States. See Brief for Appellee before the Second Circuit Court of Appeals, pp. 14-15, n. 2, *Long Island Vietnam Moratorium Comm. v. Cahn*, 437 F.2d 344 (2d Cir. 1970), *appeal docketed*, 39 U.S.L.W. 3438 (1971). The art collection of New York's Governor contains a collage of the flag with potatoes in the blue field and the Governor's picture over the stripes (Reply Brief for Appellant before the Supreme Court, p. 22, in *Radich v. New York*, 401 U.S. 531 (1971). A young man was jailed for replacing the stars by a peace symbol in his homemade American flag (Schenectady Gazette, June 6, 1970, p. 27).

23. In December 1966, Stephen Radich was prosecuted for having exhibited a series of constructions of a then unknown artist, Marc Morrel, some of which portrayed American flags in the shape of phallic symbols and other objects. His conviction under a New York statute for having cast contempt upon the American flag was affirmed by the New York courts and the Supreme Court. *People v. Radich*, 53 Misc. 2d 717, 279 N.Y.S.2d 680 (N.Y.C. Crim. Ct. 1967), *aff'd*, 26 N.Y.2d 114, 308 N.Y.S.2d 846, 257 N.E.2d 30 (1970), *aff'd by equally divided Court*, 401 U.S. 531 (1971). Justice Douglas took no part in the consideration or decision of the Supreme Court. The Court's decision in effect delays any conclusive determination of First Amendment rights to artistic works. Until the inconclusive results in the Supreme Court, it had been hoped that *Radich* would solve some of the uncertainty surrounding rights of artistic expression under the First Amendment.

More recently, three persons, now known as "The Judson Three," were arrested and charged with a variety of offenses under the New York flag desecration statute in connection with an exhibition of flag art held in November 1970 at Judson Memorial Church in Greenwich Village, New York City. In June 1971, in *People v. Hendricks*, The Judson Three were convicted. An appeal is pending.

24. See statutes cited in Ch. 7, n. 21 *supra*.

25. *Radich v. New York* (*supra* Ch. 7, n. 23).

26. *Joyce v. United States*, 259 A.2d 363 (D.C. Ct. App. 1969).

27. Associated Press Dispatch, Corning, New York, January 31, 1971.

28. *Cf. Street v. New York*, 394 U.S. 576 (1969). Ann., Constitutionality of Statutes, Ordinances, or Administrative Provisions prohibiting Defiance, Disrespect, Mutilation, or Misuse of American Flag—Federal Cases, 22 L. Ed. 2d 972 (1970).

29. *Hodsdon v. Buckson*, 310 F. Supp. 528 (D. Del. 1970); *Crosson v. Silver*, 319 F. Supp. 1084 (D. Ariz. 1970). A federal court in Arizona has ruled that flag burning is "symbolic" speech protected by the First Amendment and that a statute prohibiting such conduct is unconstitutional. *Crosson v. Silver, supra*.

30. *Radich v. New York* (*supra* Ch. 7, n. 23).

31. *United States v. Furgeson*, 302 F. Supp. 1111, 1114 (N.D. Cal. 1969). *But cf. Street v. New York*, 394 U.S. 576, 594 (1969).

32. N.Y. Gen. Bus. L. § 136 (a); 18 Penn. Stat. § 4211.

33. *Long Island Vietnam Moratorium Comm. v. Cahn, supra* note 22. *Cf. Commonwealth v. Janoff*, 439 Pa. 212, 266 A.2d 657 (1970); *Roth v. United States*, 354 U.S. 476 (1957).

34. 18 U.S.C. § 1461.

35. 19 U.S.C. § 1305 (a).

36. See, *e.g.*, Cal. Pen. Code Sec. 311.2; *Ginzburg v. U.S.*, 383 U.S. 463 (1966); *Mishkin v. N.Y.*, 383 U.S. 502 (1966).

37. See, *e.g.*, N.Y. Pen. L. §§ 235.00 (4), 235.05 (1).

38. *Roth v. United States* (*supra* Ch. 7, n. 33) p. 483.

39. *Memoirs v. Massachusetts*, 383 U.S. 413, 418 (1966).

40. N.Y. Pen. L. § 235.00 (1).

41. *Ginzburg v. United States*, 383 U.S. 463 (1966).

42. *Ibid.*

43. *United States v. Ginzburg*, 224 F. Supp. 129 (E.D. Pa., 1963), *aff'd*, 338 F.2d 12 (3d Cir. 1964), *aff'd*, 383 U.S. 463 (1966).

44. *Ginsberg v. New York*, 390 U.S. 629 (1968).

45. N.Y. Pen. L. § 235.21.

46. See *People v. Gonzales*, 107 N.Y.S.2d 968 (N.Y.C. Magis. Ct. 1951); *People v. Vanguard Press, Inc.*, 192 Misc. 127, 84 N.Y.S.2d 427 (N.Y.C. Magis. Ct. 1947).

47. *N.Y. Times Co. v. Sullivan*, 376 U.S. 254 (1964).

48. *Burton v. Cromwell Pub. Co.*, 82 F.2d 154 (2d Cir. 1936).

49. *Monson v. Tussauds Ltd.*, [1894] 1 Q.B. 671, 63 L.J.Q.B. 454.

50. *Zbyszko v. N.Y. American, Inc.*, 228 App. Div. 277, 239 N.Y.S. 411 (1st Dept. 1930).

51. *Beauharnais v. Illinois*, 343 U.S. 259 (1952); the continuing vitality of this decision was questioned by Judge Wright in his concurring opinion in *Anti-Defamation League of B'nai B'rith, Pac. S. W. Reg. O.V. FCC.* (D.C. Cir., 1968) 403 F. 2d 169 *cert. den.*, 394 U.S. 930, 1969.

52. *Schutzman & Schutzman v. News Syndicate Co.*, 60 Misc. 2d 827, 304 N.Y.S.2d 167 (Sup. Ct. Nassau Co. 1969).

53. W. Prosser, *Torts* 636-37 (2d ed. 1955).

54. Silver, *Privacy and the First Amendment*, 34 Fordham L. Rev. 553 (1966); see, *e.g.*, N.Y. Civ. Rights L. §§ 50-5¹.

55. *Freed v. Loew's Inc.*, 175 Misc. 616, 24 N.Y.S.2d 679 (Sup. Ct. Bronx Co. 1940).

56. 175 Misc. 616, 617, 24 N.Y.S.2d 679, 680.

57. *Young v. Greneker Studios, Inc.*, 175 Misc. 1027, 26 N.Y.S.2d 357 (Sup. Ct. N.Y. Co. 1941).

58. *Neyland v. Home Pattern Co.*, 65 F.2d 363 (2d Cir. 1933) (L. Hand, J.), *cert. den.*, 290 U.S. 661 (1934).

59. *Rosenbloom v. Metromedia, Inc.*, 403 U.S. 29 (1971); *N.Y. Times Co. v. Sullivan*, 376 U.S. 254 (1964); *Time, Inc. v. Hill*, 385 U.S. 374 (1967); *Spahn v. Julian Messner, Inc.*, 21 N.Y.2d 124, 286 N.Y.S.2d 832 (1967), *app. dism'd*, 393 U.S. 1046 (1968).

60. *Ibid.*

61. *Walker v. D'Alesandro*, 212 Md. 163, 180, 129 A.2d 148, 157 (1957). (Held that defendant Mayor of Baltimore was not entitled to an absolute privilege barring the action.)

62. *Battersby v. Collier*, 34 App. Div. 347, 353-54, 54 N.Y.S. 363, 368 (1st Dept. 1898).

63. *Neyland v. Home Pattern Co.*, *supra* note 228.

64. *Cf. id.* at 364, 365.

65. The last sentence of the New York invasion of privacy statute provides explicitly that "nothing contained in this act shall be so construed as to prevent any person . . . from using the name . . . of any . . . artist in connection with his . . . artistic productions which he has sold or disposed of with such name . . . used in connection therewith." N.Y. Civ. Rights L. § 51.

CHAPTER 8

1. Cal. Civ. Code § 1740.

2. N.Y. Gen. Bus. L. Art. 12-C, § 219-a.

3. 1969 N.Y. State Legis. Annual 92, at 93.

4. N.Y. Gen. Bus. L. Art. 12-F.

5. N.Y. Gen. Bus. L. Art. 22-A, ¶349 (b) and N.Y. Exec. L. Art. 5, ¶63[12].

6. N.Y. Gen. Bus. L. Art. 12-D.

7. See *State v. Wright Hepburn Webster Gallery, Ltd. et al.*, 64 Misc. 2d 423 (Sup. N.Y. 1970). However, this case does not prohibit an artist from executing works in the style of another.

8. 1968 N.Y. State Legis. Annual 78, at 79. For a discussion of this statute and a comparison to an analogous statute enacted in England, see Feldman, *New Protection for the Art Collector—Warranties, Opinions and Disclaimers* in The Record of The Association of The Bar of the City of New York, 661 *et seq.* (December 1968). See recent case, *Weisz v. Parke-Bernet Galleries, Inc.*, 67 Misc.2d 1077, 325 N.Y.S.2d 576 (Civ. Ct., 1971).

9. N.Y. Gen. Bus. L. Art. 12-E.

10. 287 N.Y. 302, 39 N.E.2d 249 (1942).

11. The Court of Appeals in the *Pushman* case refused to treat the question as to whether the artist by his sale of the painting *and* a subsequent public exhibition may have "published" the work so as to lose his common law copyright. 287 N.Y. 302, 308, 39 N.E.2d 249, 251. If the work were not published, the common law rights of copyright may be broader than federal statutory copyright. See *Nimmer, supra* Ch. 1, n. 2, § 111. Commentators have always reacted hesitatingly as to when "publication" of a painting occurs. See, for example, *Cahn, supra* Ch. 1, n. 5, p.3: ". . . the exhibition of a painting in a gallery to which the public is admitted and where copying is not prohibited, may be publication of the picture. . . ;" *Price, supra* Ch. 1, n. 28. For a recent extensive discussion as to whether exhibition of an artwork constitutes publication, see Jonakait, *Do Art Exhibitions Destroy Commonlaw Copyright in Works of Art?*, published in ASCAP Copyright L. Symp. (Nathan Burkan Memorial Competition, 1969), 81 *et seq.*

12. 1966 N.Y. State Legis. Annual 30a.

13. See *Nimmer* §§ 1, 93.3.

14. 17 U.S.C. § 2. The Copyright Revision Bill which was pending in 1971 [S.644, 92d Cong., 1st Sess. (1971)] would have eliminated state jurisdiction over common law copyright in all but certain instances. Section 301 of the Bill proposes a dual test to determine whether state power has been pre-empted by Congress: any rights under state law (whether common law or statutory) would be abolished if they 1) are equivalent to copyright and 2) extend to works coming within the scope of the federal copyright law. Determining the equivalency to copyright of nominally different state-protected rights is a difficult task. See Goldstein, *Federal System Ordering of The Copyright Interest*, 69 Colum. L. Rev. 49, 53 (1969).

15. This conclusion is consistent with the discussion contained in the pamphlet prepared by Joshua Binion Cahn for Artists Equity Association prior to the enactment of the New York statutes (see *Cahn, [supra* Ch. 1, n. 5], p. 3) where he points out that "even if the copyright notice has been affixed the reproduction rights should always be specifically reserved in writing."

16. It has been suggested, however, that as a result of the listing of permissible reproductions as set forth in the legislative purpose clause of the New York statute (L. 1966, c. 668, § 1) the right of reproduction under New York common law copyright is narrower than the comparable right under statutory copyright. See *Nimmer, supra* Ch. 1, n. 2, Ch. 10, notes 179e and 179f. Not to be overlooked, however, by any lawyer engaged in depth in the problem is the potential impact of the United States Supreme Court landmark cases in *Sears, Roebuck & Co. v. Stiffel Co.* (376 U.S. 225 (1964)) and *Compco Corp. v. Day-Brite Lighting, Inc.* (376 U.S. 234 (1964)), which repudiated a state's rules of unfair competition that "touches upon the area" of the federal patent and copyright statutes. See, *e.g., Goldstein (supra* Ch. 8, n. 14), 62 *et seq.* An extensive discussion of the implication of these decisions is beyond the scope of this monograph.

17. N.Y. Gen. Bus. L. Art. 12-G.

18. 1968 N.Y. State Legis. Annual 82, at 83.

INDEX

TABLE OF CASES